Inner Peace

The Soul Self
Remembered

Dr. Karon Lobrovich

Channel for André

André's Whispers Publishing
Flagstaff, Arizona

ॐ

Published by André's Whispers Publishing
2700 S. Woodlands Village Blvd.
Suite 300-409
Flagstaff, Arizona 86001
www.andreswhispers.com

Cover design by: John Lobrovich
Art Work by: Denise & Mike Bruck

Library of Congress Cataloging-in-Publication Data
TXu 1-792-671 January 24, 2012

ISBN: 978-0-578-09718-3

ॐ

Introduction

The following is a collection of topics intended to be used as weekly meditations. The readers are invited by the collective of loving guides, André, to open their lives to new possibilities of creating a peaceful and flowing existence.

This guidance assists in developing a healthy partnership between the Personality Self and the Soul Self. The new relationship of expanded Consciousness will help produce a life path that brings joy and peace to daily life.

The change in your life occurs as you replace old thought processes with new thoughts and actions in response to what is happening around you. You learn how to see the real energy of a situation and become transparent to energies that are not a positive addition to your experience.

We hope that this work becomes a means of developing the connection you have always dreamed of and the faith that it is possible to have a life experience immersed in peace and understanding.

ॐ

Contents

Preface | 8

1
You Asked for the Search to End | 15

2
Your Total, Complete Perfection | 18

3
Each Path is Unique | 21

4
Remove the Fog | 24

5
Take it Slow | 26

6
Maintaining the Connection | 29

7
Set Aside the Necessary Time | 31

8
Develop Your Life | 33

9
Play with the Now | 36

10
Heed What You Hear | 39

11
Build Your Watchtower | 41

ॐ

Contents

12
The Journey is What it is All About | 45

13
You Are the Power | 49

14
You as Part of the Greater Whole | 51

15
The Peaceful Heart | 53

16
Change What You Create | 56

17
Drama and the Ego | 58

18
The Ramblings of the Mind | 63

19
What Do You Really Want? | 67

20
Creating a Peaceful Flow | 69

21
Add Comfort to the Body | 72

22
Allow Others to Be | 74

ॐ

Contents

23
Are They Really Doing Their Best? | 76

24
Balance Earth and Soul | 79

25
Become Sensitive to Your Path | 81

26
Blend the Personality and Soul Self | 85

27
Broadening the View | 88

28
Become the Stillness | 90

29
The Choices We Make | 92

30
Creating Balance in Your Life | 95

31
Helping Others | 98

32
Why Do You Want to Help? | 102

33
Cultivate Clarity | 103

ॐ

Contents

34
Dealing with Issues of Abandonment | 107

35
Develop Self-Love | 109

36
Reducing the Downward Spiral | 112

37
Judgment Based on Frequency | 115

38
Expanding Your Vision | 118

39
Find the Trigger | 121

40
Formulation of Thought | 124

41
Get the Most Out of This Existence | 127

42
Growing Too Fast | 129

43
Healthy Connection | 132

44
How Do I Love? | 135

ॐ

Contents

45
Positive Creative Nature | 138

46
It's About the Effort Involved | 141

47
Keep the Flow | 144

48
Change the Turmoil | 147

49
Knowledge at Your Fingertips | 149

50
Life as an Illusion | 153

51
What Went Wrong? | 155

52
Listen to Your Thoughts | 157

53
Personal Growth | 160

54
Reasoning and Change | 164

55
What is Faith? | 167

ॐ

Contents

56
Resonate With the Essence | 169

57
Where Did the Flow Go? | 172

58
What is the Pull of the Future? | 175

59
Selecting the Experience | 178

60
Why Did I Do That? | 180

61
Stay in the Moment | 184

62
The False Belief System | 187

63
The Fluid Nature of Things | 190

64
Where Are You in Your Growth? | 193

65
The Root Source of Emotion | 196

66
See the Blessing in Chaos | 198

ॐ

Contents

67
View Life from the Soul Level | 202

68
Reduce the Tentacles | 205

69
Setting the Frequency in Advance | 209

70
Seeing the Oneness in All | 213

71
The "Isness" of the Energy | 215

72
Using Multiple View Points | 219

73
Offering Advice to Others | 221

74
What Is Love? | 225

75
Be Your Own Master | 227

Glossary | 230

ॐ

Preface

I offer this book to you in the hopes that it will illuminate your soul's journey and assist in understanding the role you play in creating your life. As I put this book together, I was asked how it all came about, and I want to tell you that story as it began over 20 years ago. Here is the beginning of how that seed got planted, and how the process of collecting the lessons ensued. It began with my irritation at missing sleep, but ends with this beautiful book in your hands.

In 1999 I began writing the passages for this book out of desperation to get a good night's sleep. I was awakened by the sound of persistent words and phrases in my head. This occurred nightly around 1 a.m., nagging at me for hours at a time. I attempted to silence the voice but I gave up and was drawn to get up and record what I was hearing. The words originated from an energy source that I was unable to see or touch but I found the experience natural,

ॐ

completely loving and gracious. This was the beginning of the channeling experience that changed my life.

In preparation for the night time writing I kept a notebook and pen near my meditation pillow. This way I could stumble half asleep to my meditation room, sit on my zafu cushion and invite the flow of information to begin. Each evening I would scribble approximately two pages of phrases and concepts. Transcribing the information was challenging because some of the times I heard specific phrases and other times I was given an entire concept to record. Each session lasted about thirty minutes and ended with kind words such as, "You are loved," "Peace be with you" or words of thanks. Occasionally the ending words referenced my night time fatigue and that we should end our conversation.

It was disturbing to be awakened every night, and I wondered if there was a reason that the rendezvous had to be at 1 a.m. I experimented with a more convenient time by sitting down with my notebook and pen at 7 p.m. The words came as I learned how to quiet myself more deeply. Eventually I was able to

ॐ

connect with this guidance any time of day, and only on the days it was convenient. The relationship grew into one of mutual trust and admiration. It became more streamline and sophisticated. I could choose when to write and was no longer nudged to pick up my pen. It was as if the energy source was confident that I would come back for more information.

Hearing voices was not new to me. As a 3-year-old I saw entities and received guidance from them. This continued into adulthood in the form of visual, auditory and empathic events. In an effort to find meaning for the confusing experiences, I began meditating. Meditation helped me balance the day-to-day issues created by working full time and having a family. I dedicated a small area of the house to my practice of meditation and on days that I did not feel like mediating, I found myself gravitating there to relax and regroup.

Meditation created a stable environment to travel as a spectator and student. I craved clarity about the relationship between what I saw in the mirror each morning and what I experienced during meditation. I wanted more. The energies and relationships I

ॐ

experienced during meditation were genuine, but the memory of their existence faded as I stepped into my Earth roles.

I asked, "How do I blend the two seemingly opposite existences? How can I embody a life of peace and joy while encased in an environment of turmoil and chaos? Are the two life paths mutually exclusive? Why is it that I am allowed access to a state that is flowing and fulfilling only to return time and time again to the same energies that I left? How can I retain this feeling of clarity all day? Am I engaged in someone's sick comedy or am I simply being teased?"

My questions persisted until I began writing. I believe the barrage of questions I posed initiated the appearance of the energy source. I don't think I would have been given the opportunity to channel this information if not for my consistent practice of meditation.

The information given to me is focused on creating a balance between the Personality-Self and Soul-Self. The terminology is slightly different than what many of us are accustom.

ॐ

However, the resulting education I received was amazing. This book answers the questions I presented.

After years of writing these passages a new question came to mind.

I asked the guide, "What should I call you? Do you have a name?"

The response came, "We understand why you are requesting a name, but a name is not necessary."

I repeated the request for a name and was shown the name André in my mind, with an acute accent above the "e." André is a collective voice and an essence who is not bound by one identity or personality. As I channel the voice, it is a source of wisdom given to me by "we." The pronoun "me" to identify the voice is not used, which informs me André is a collective soul, a cooperative essence.

I housed the notebooks, loose papers and journals filled with the channeled passages in my meditation room unused and undeveloped. However, as I visited with friends and listened to the struggles they were facing, I remembered the channeled passages. This prompted me to type the passages so

ॐ

my friends could read them. I was thrilled that they were able to comprehend the methods of bringing the Soul's messages into their lives. This is how I began the journey to share the collection of André's wisdom.

The beautiful passages continued to flow on paper. It came as no surprise when André talked about sharing the passages with other people. The following is what I heard one day: "We want the passages accessible to others with the full feeling of Love. It must always be held sacred. This work does not judge. It cannot. It must be presented through passionate, loving and honest connection with others."

I believe the loving and non-judgmental nature of the information is what sets it apart from other personality growth books. I have created a beautiful flowing and joyful life by remembering to listen to the guidance of my Soul Self. The wisdom in *Inner Peace* makes it easy to continually grow in a loving harmonious direction.

I hope you find this book an exciting resource to help you grow in the most peace-filled direction

ॐ

possible. I wish Love and Light to you and your joyous path.

Dr. Karon Lobrovich

ॐ

1

You Asked for the Search to End

The most important concept to remember at all times is that you are as exactly as you should be. Exactly the way you are, without changing anything about yourself. Through this work you have simply chosen to be more aware of your Soul's nature, to be more fluid in your connection with the All-That-Is, in an effort to live a more peaceful life. You are able to do this in all your current perfection.

This search is a craving for the truth hidden deep within. The only change you may elect to do is to modify some habits you developed in response to the lower energies existing around you. The habits have

ॐ

kept your vision cloudy and your felt sense overwhelmed by lower energy. This does not mean you are any less perfect. Perfection, or the lack of it, is a human thought process. You are simply a pure Being – that is all.

You are a pure Being that is exposed to a variety of situations, energies and other forms of stimuli. If you choose to be distracted by this phenomenon, so be it. That path is also a value. However, we feel that you are being called to remember and, in doing that, you are choosing to integrate the past Universal experiences with your present experiences. This is a choice you made quite some time ago. In doing this, you may succeed in fully integrating your current habits with the Universal knowledge base. You may choose to integrate all or some of this information. The outcome will be just what you, and only you, feel is right.

You have asked for help in sorting out what the Personality Self does in response to conditions around you. You have asked for assistance in modifying your manifestations.

🕉

So we offer assistance – advice. But you are the driving force behind this. You wanted this integration, not as a form to create stress, but as a joyful celebration of life in the beautiful Earth-level plane. By integrating and seeing, feeling and knowing the Oneness in all that you experience, you are manifesting the highest state here for you and the others around you. It becomes a form of devotion that you are able to take part in, purely by choice.

A state of awareness is what you will focus on with this work. The work is not designed to point out imperfections in yourself or others. It will assist your heart in experiencing a wonderful state in as many different surrounding circumstances as possible, thereby bringing the Oneness to the forefront. As that vibration is activated and you are in awareness of that state, the intensity of the experience is significantly increased.

When your daily focus becomes a search for the highest vibration in all moments, you gain the ability to influence a larger area than you currently can. You increase your ability to send out the highest form of Love.

ॐ

2

Your Total, Complete Perfection

It is very exciting to watch your growth as you relearn what you have forgotten. It is to us the same as when you watch a young child learn to navigate the world. There are always messages you wish they would hear deep in their hearts and never forget. There are roads you want them to avoid, situations you wish they would bypass, but ultimately you know that they will make the final choices and thereby create their own future.

The natural pace, at which most of you take in your existence and meet internal and external challenges, is a wonder to watch. It is what you are

ॐ

not able to see that influences you and makes you feel inferior to the larger scheme of things. This is an occurrence that we, in the spiritual plane, wish we could influence more than any of the other habits we see developing. The habits of self-doubt, self-hatred and self-abuse are creators of low frequency energy.

Your experiences can be used as tools for learning, but we see that some of you hold yourself hostage over your previous painful actions. This causes you to relive painful memories. It is not necessary for you to do so, but the Ego thrives on it. The Ego wants to prolong the "feeling" aspect of a situation that you experienced by reliving or escalating the intensity of the feelings you experienced. That is a form of "piggy backing" on the initial energy.

If you have an undesirable experience that your mind revisits repeatedly, notice how the thoughts are accompanied by intense negative feelings. The negative feelings are what you Ego is addicted to. By using the skills in these meditations you can learn to choose to stop and say "no more." You will learn new thoughts that bring you pleasure until the lure of

ॐ

the past is completely replaced with the feelings of love or joy. Joy is the natural state of the Soul, and the more you can replace any feeling of less than peace, joy or love, the easier you will find your upward growth. Remember that every thought you have is one of either an upward swing or a downward swing. Keep your thoughts happy or on the upward swing!

ॐ

3

Each Path is Unique

There is a way to select your path or choice of direction to proceed in your life. You may feel that all individuals need to follow the same path, but actually each of you will have your own desires, personality traits and life situations that will affect your decisions. This individualism is what makes each Soul growth an experience unlike any other. The process is the important piece. Rather than attempting to hurry to a fixed goal, we recommend that you focus on where you are now, in order that you may enjoy and thus learn about your situations as they manifest themselves.

ॐ

Each of you has infinite ability to create an environment that only you could or would want to create. Each has his own taste, likes and dislikes, as well as preferences of thought patterns that would not be attractive to another. This is part of the plan. There are many ways to manifest and they are all perfectly flowing, no matter how far off you may feel they are. Individual patterns of growth are as special as each snowflake that falls from the sky. The snowflake pattern is unique, as well as the path it chooses to fall from the cloud. One path is not superior to another.

This Earth-level setting creates a myriad of possibilities for the human experience. It was initiated in such a way so that each Soul would be set free in a boundless set of circumstances and a plethora of actions and re-actions to any given moment. It is important to focus on maintaining your personal balance, which will help you manage your life and not focus on the actions of others. Without the proper focus, you would not be able to objectively attempt this type of growth, even in the most rudimentary manner.

ॐ

The glow from each of you is so very special, each individual has his or her own signature, making one of the most beautiful and inspiring visualizations for us. We are continually amazed with the wonderful combinations you develop and then expand. Perhaps one day, you will remember what it looks like to observe the Light, so that you will be able to see it with your Soul's eyes! We all share in the growth together, and it is a very joyful experience.

ॐ

4

Remove the Fog

You are always engulfed in Spirit. It is impossible for you to truly separate yourself from the Divinity within you. Some of your actions may not reflect that connection, but in any state you are still one with the All-That-Is. You may experience such strong emotional energy from your Ego, that even if you stop and look for the connection, you will not readily see it. The Ego has been using low frequency vibration in humankind for thousands of years and is comfortable with its existence. You are attempting to wake up, so to speak, and find the other realities that

ॐ

are sitting just under the surface of your Egoistic mind.

If you choose to maintain this level of awareness, there will be a short struggle to "keep your head above the fog." It will only require a few minutes each day to focus your energy. Then, throughout the day, it will be necessary to still the mind for a few seconds to feel or remember the connection. This periodic reconnecting is an imperative part of this process.

The reawakening of your true self is what you are learning. It is natural that you seek joy and peace. We will help you learn to apply this knowledge to your daily existence. What comes with this is a true sense of comfort, lightness of heart and connection with others. When you are able to live in this state, you will attract into your life the relationships, situations and experiences which will continue to open your heart and amaze your Ego.

ॐ

5

Take it Slow

When we ask you to adjust the habits you use to cope with daily life, what we are saying is simply try something new. Don't think of it as a dreary task to be completed. Take this instruction as a welcomed challenge, something you do with joy and curiosity. If you set it up in negative light, you are going to be prone to failure or becoming overwhelmed. Don't be so serious about getting it "right" the first time you work with these new ideas. Spiritual development should be a joyful, rewarding experience. After all, this quest is undertaken to fill a void that is craved by the Spirit. It is not a task of gloom and despair.

ॐ

When you observe with the attitude of love and joy, you can have fun and see the humor in your previous ways. You don't expect children to grow overnight, do you? Why would you expect an adult to change a habit overnight without experiencing setbacks or bouts of fear and forgetfulness?

This work will challenge all the various aspects of your Personality Self. Some aspects may be able to work with these new concepts without difficulty and resistance, but once in a while an emotion will be triggered and you may fall back into a habit. The moment you realize that something is wrong or you know you are not centered, stop and observe. There is no reason to become a judge and look to place blame. Just observe the ongoing situation by the emotion and feelings you have. That means to be careful not to manifest a re-action. Simply pull back to the side as the Soul Self and see the situation as energy.

This may take seconds or it may take a day! But you will not be able to continue with action in a healthy manner while you are confused, fearful or full

ॐ

of the emotion that temporarily pulled you from your center.

Be respectful of this situation for it holds pearls of great learning. It may help to do something preplanned when this occurs, such as using a mantra, going to a special place or sitting quietly. This will help you turn off the re-action response and turn on the observation behavior.

ॐ

6

Maintaining the Connection

When you think about the way people make choices, you can see an enormous variability in humankind. This is because many people completely shut off their inner guidance. Others listen occasionally and some cultivate the habit of maintaining a connection. It is not that all people would behave in the exact same manner if they were connected to Spirit. Each person has his own goals and ideas of the best way to experience the gifts offered in the Earth plane.

People who are maintaining that connection appear calmer and less engaged with day-to-day

ॐ

drama. As the skill of maintaining the connection is developed, you are able to "pick-up" the emotions of others. This provides new opportunities or challenges regarding your own insecurities. It will require that you develop the confidence, trust and passion to continue on your chosen path. Fear of criticism or fear of not being accepted by friends and family can become a deterrent.

To cope with this, it is necessary to develop the ability to consistently see the words and actions of yourself and others as energy. It is also wise to work on eliminating all forms of re-action in your day-to-day life. To Be the Peace of God, requires that you release the re-active defense to words and release the fear of losing control.

ॐ

7

Set Aside the Necessary Time

Being is another name for awareness, awareness of the connection to your Higher Self. You will always have a connection, but the actual variable lies in the strength or ease of the connection. Just as an athlete understands the significance of repeated, structured practice, so must one who is intent on developing or fine tuning this connection with the Source.

Talk with yourself; see what is core to you. What do you really want? If the connection is really important to you, then be prepared to set regular time aside to be still. You will need to learn to

ॐ

observe the times when that connection becomes challenged. Look at the challenging situation as a gift, see the area you want to change and then let it go! Apply what you learn little by little.

Your choice to do this is what will set you apart from those who study and surround themselves with spiritual objects and books, but who are unwilling to apply the knowledge in their day-to-day lives.

ॐ

8

Develop Your Life

The only difference between you and another individual is the space you occupy. You both are composed of the same light or energy, but each person is working to have unique individual experiences. In other words, Source does not set Universal patterns of behavior or experiences, even at the Soul level. In this respect, there is no entity that functions as a puppeteer in the heavens manipulating a Soul or personality. It is more like initiating movement in smoke with your hand and observing all the patterns that develop on their own. This movement can be thought of as life experiences. You

ॐ

would not be able to look at sections of a "swirl" in the smoke and from that infer what the entire pattern would look like. The same holds true for an individual existence.

The momentum individuals set up for themselves is a significant factor in initiating experiences. For instance, take the choice of an education over minimal or no education - the life experiences will differ dramatically. This is also true for the work/play environment chosen and even the family life or location to live on the Earth-level plane. There are enormous variables to consider as a person chooses the future path and modifies it one decision at a time. This is influenced by mood, past experience and external pressures. Be careful not to feel trapped in a lifestyle or single life influence. Each situation should be perceived as a teacher and can be the beginning to a new way of life.

By using the process previously described, you can observe your path and call in your higher guidance. This will direct your perspective of each situation appropriately, and allow you to make choices that support the outcome you desire. You

ॐ

have the ability to "control" or influence this path more than you are aware. As a child, you may have attempted to control an outcome of a situation without understanding the result you wanted. This may have convinced you that you had little or no control. Actually, you were experiencing the results of your previous desires or choices. You were unaware of the momentum you set prior to focusing on one wish that may have been out of sequence with the others.

You are able to initiate change in almost any direction and it would be prudent to practice this on a daily basis. See where you are headed, look at the desires of the path that lies deep inside, and set your intent in that direction. After you do this, release the outcome or control of your intent to the powers that be and watch the results. Know and trust that the outcome is for your highest good and will align with the larger path you chose long ago.

ॐ

9

Play with the Now

Wouldn't it be nice if the only area of concern for you was a singular moment, and you were able to focus on this very moment, free of past or future thoughts? If you had only this moment, full of its sensations and feelings, you would be able to take advantage of expanding what you were in the presence of!

You don't practice that very often because you are so "busy" with the forces of past and future. This limits what you are able to hold in your awareness during this present moment. Focusing on the past or future are habits you developed as a child, such as

ॐ

waiting until you are ten years old so you can feel like a big kid or "you just wait until your father gets home!"

You are taught this. You are taught that you should sit and put thought and energy into a situation before it arrives so that you will be better prepared. The reality is that many times this thought becomes worry; the mind adds new and different scenarios to the upcoming situation. This can become entertainment for your Ego. You are able to imagine wonderful or terrible outcomes. You also can sit for hours thinking about something from the past and replay it in your head over and over until you feel either the joy or the intense fear or pain, you felt during a situation. The Ego loves this type of entertainment.

The only way to focus on actual joy is to be in the present moment. Be fully aware of your body, your surroundings and your feelings. Take advantage of this state and learn to project more loving and satisfying energy into all facets of your life. Feel the energy and its flow, its vibration and its calm, loving light. When you are in a state of accepting the present

ॐ

moment, you can "grow" the feeling and have it encompass you. This aware state can be with you at work or home. It will assist you in decision-making, physical movement and emotional flow. When you practice opening yourself to this state on a regular basis, you will significantly influence your environment and project a higher form of energy into it.

When you focus for long periods of time on the past or future, you are not in an upward flow. Instead, you are playing with an illusion that will not allow you the freedom of growth. It is an energy that causes unnecessary worry and tension. Your Ego remembers how it felt in the past and it wants to feel alive by playing with the thoughts over and over.

Stay in the moment and play with the experience at hand. Bring as many joyful feelings into what you are now doing and, in doing so you will attract more joyful experiences into your life.

ॐ

10

Heed What You Hear

Your Truth is what you usually abide by, but when stress enters your life, you have brushed your Truth away and taken on another's beliefs. Your fear rules what you do and say, rather than allowing Love and Truth to be the deciding factor. In these situations, you do not trust your guidance as it applies to you.

It is easy to see Truth for those around you at a distance. However, when the issues affect you, you skew them so they favor another at your own expense. This is done at the personality level.

ॐ

Stand fast. Listen to what is offered and heed the advice. Do this consistently to obtain the most upward flow in your life.

ॐ

11

Build Your Watchtower

Putting trust in what you feel is right is not easy to do consistently. Many people begin with wonderful plans, but then allow fear to creep in. The plans suddenly become too daunting, and the process that at first seemed exciting becomes laborious and heavy. What changed? Did the plan or dream change? No, but a few things did occur. You began with excitement and, when that energy needed recharging, you filled that space with just a little doubt, rather than going to your Source energy and recharging. You filled the mental space with fear thoughts -

ॐ

thoughts that asked what if, or how - or doubt that you are not good enough for the plans.

There is a predictive reason this occurs. Your Ego, which desires conflict, creates it! It wants to be noticed. The Ego feels left out when you are focused on flow, goodness and production of a desire that does not include stress, fear and negative vibrations. It wants attention! "Notice me! Remember things do not come easily for you. You are ALWAYS let down in one form or fashion." When you hear these old thoughts playing in your head, doubt creeps in and it can cascade into a total feeling of defeat.

If this occurs, all is not lost. It is just another opportunity to remember that old habits stay around awhile and that a portion of your energy will need to be allocated to setting up the "watchtower." Fill the watchtower with loving and self-confident feelings. These feelings can watch to see if you begin to waver from your initial path. The watchtower is the energy you set aside, up high enough to see your progress from afar, so that energy flowing around you does not consume it. It is able to see through the fog, so to speak. To utilize this energy, check in with the tower

ॐ

routinely when things are going well, and visit hourly when things in your life are rocky. When you visit, you are honoring yourself as well as the Higher Self you have assigned for the job.

So, what do you do if you have not already set up a "watchtower" of energy? Start one now. Find a visualization of a place or room that makes you feel safe, then go visit and discuss what you want to happen. What are your routine habits? How can this energy source warn you when it notices the slightest wavering from the course? What will be your signal to the watchtower if you find yourself in trouble? Set up a plan in your mind while visiting the tower of energy. Cover all the angles you can think of. Run through a few scenarios and, using the signal you chose, see it working. Feel how good it is to have this safety net at your disposal. Play here until you feel good again. This will help you get ready to jump back into the Earth-level dream with a renewed sense of enthusiasm and energy!

Remember to visit the tower routinely to be recharged before your "battery" becomes too low. When you visit, you are concurrently recharging the

ॐ

tower for your next visit. The more you visit the tower, the sandy pathway becomes easier to find. That way, when you feel very dark, you will be able to see your path. You will be on autopilot and will not need to put any effort into finding your tower!

ॐ

12

The Journey is What it is All About

You as an entity create your life in this environment right now. You are in a location that offers you a myriad of sources, materials and stimulations, which can give rise to your growth. You can create comfort right here and now with all the talents seen and unseen that you have already cultivated. Don't think that you should put off your growth until you reach another phase in this life.

If you feel drawn to increase your awareness, take advantage of the focus you do have and begin to play with these suggestions. Become one with your process of growth. Fall in love with the path, fall in

ॐ

love with your new thoughts and even the small ideas you have. There is much truth to the saying "Life is not a destination but a journey." The journey is the color, texture and sensation. Take this as success and joyfully proceed to focus on your new adventure. Each adventure requires focus, energy and an open mind. The journey is what it is all about.

You have the choice to continue the amazing growth or become complacent with any given choices you are presented with. Do you find that you direct your life toward one of slow or very little growth? Are you even aware that you made those choices? Look at an area in your life in which you feel less than successful. It could be that you feel you are not good at sports, cooking, singing, math, money management or even creating positive experiences. Just select one and sit with it for a moment or so. When did you first feel you were not good at it? Did someone tell you or did you decide that you were not good at it for yourself? Do you like to identify yourself as someone who does poorly at this topic? When you chose to see yourself as not doing well,

🕉

was it because it seemed not to come easily to you? Perhaps it is just not in your nature?

You can grab an old thought process, such as one you just found, and hold it while you are sitting quietly and surround it with an image of beautiful light. Any color will do, but it needs to be one that you enjoy. Have the color begin to move around the topic (or a visual of you doing the action). Continue to circulate the color and modify it as you feel drawn. Have the color permeate the objects, go around, though and blend completely with the action or object until the entire picture is a beautiful sight. There may now be enough beauty in your old thought process so that you are drawn to go there to experience this state filled with new energy.

This is a talent you have. This area can now be something you enjoy doing or being part of. You can repeat this process any time you "lose" the feeling to a lower energy flow. Repeat it as a shorter version just to boost your energy for the topic. After a while, you will not need to do this because your basic energy pattern will change. Once this change occurs, you can pick a new area to play with. This is the

ॐ

journey and the path; and all of it is in the here and now for you to stand up and notice. Become one with it and enjoy the grand adventure!

ॐ

13

You Are the Power

You are the creator of your own joys, sorrows and experiences. Once you realize this you can escape from the bonds of the illusion that external objects or persons or even conditions *cause* your life to unfold. Long ago, you asked for a set of circumstances to work with during your life. You are the director and main character of this play.

You have the power of the Source within and the power to change the momentum of your life into whatever you are capable of seeing occur. Your true limitation is within rather than without. You must choose to release the fear that renders you

ॐ

motionless. There is an abundance of motion, creativity and love within your Being, today, as you are at this moment. Your fear is your only wall, the only barrier between you and a total experience. A life!

A life of joy and pain – in balance

A life of celebration and struggle – in balance

A life of wonder and contentment – in perfect balance

ॐ

14

You as Part of the Greater Whole

The energy patterns, the Soul development and, even the seemingly dysfunctional behaviors are all part of the greater whole. You can't isolate yourself into a Being independent of the influence of others. You are one with the All-That-Is. You are one with all of life - so live it! Observe it closely enough so you can create what you think you would enjoy. After observing, you can create it again into the new idea of what you would enjoy. That is the beauty - the continuous change - the continual opportunity to learn what you can do for yourself and others. You have a wide range of influence, even in areas in which

ॐ

you are unaware. The energy you create and modify touches many others in ways you do not understand. Be respectful of this.

It is advantageous to continue to keep your behaviors, thoughts and yearnings focused on activities that will enhance your life in a manner that is pleasing to you. Your joy can radiate through many planes and will resonate new life into previously undirected vibration. This joyful energy will assist mankind as it shifts into a higher vibration. As you become aware of your connection, ready to consistently express oneness with other life forms, you will receive support from them. You will feel the difference and so will those around you. Focus your attention on actions that help make you feel lighter and less burdened. If you concentrate in that direction, you will find that your path becomes filled with joy and peace.

ॐ

15

The Peaceful Heart

We want to help you understand what it means to have peace in your heart. The amount of peace you maintain at any given time is determined by the current state of flow you are experiencing. This means that if you increase the amount of flow you feel, you will also increase your perceived level of peace. The two go hand in hand. So, if you feel that you are obtaining flow in most aspects of your life, but do not feel at peace, then you are probably not really obtaining, or at least maintaining, true flow.

What is the flow we are speaking of? It is vibration or energy that you manage. It includes the

ॐ

energy inside your body, as well as the energy just outside your physical body. You can learn to calm the mind enough to begin to alter your state of awareness and learn to maintain this state long enough to actually shift the energy around your body. You will begin to feel a flow and when flow is maintained then peace will be at the forefront of your life.

Most of the time people move in and out of flow. Some people stay in the flow longer than others, but most do not maintain this state for extended periods of time. If you truly want to experience peace in your life, you must learn to maintain the necessary state of flow to influence your energy body. The energy body is made up of all of your various attitudes, opinions, and other thought processes.

Your energy body began when you came into your body and has been growing since that time. By awareness and focus, you can shift the entire paradigm in which you live. By shifting the frequency of what you emit, you will be able to change everything you attract into your life. This will assist you in realizing your dream of a peaceful life.

ॐ

A peaceful heart is one that does not worry about situations. That individual simply makes an observation and will either choose action or inaction. It is truly a moment-to-moment interpretation of the daily activities in which one can be involved. Peace or flow meanders in and out of all events. A bystander may perceive the full flowing energies you radiate. A person in the flow or one with a peaceful heart will influence the activities around them to such an extent that they may rarely perceive conflict any more. The situations in their life will consistently flow without intentional interference. Their ability to avoid stress or negative situations becomes second nature. That individual will simply say "why would I want to expose myself to such?" So they don't.

ॐ

16

Change What You Create

What would you like to do? Are you interested in any particular change or are you simply realizing that what you are practicing now is not working for you? You may simply realize that you are not comfortable any more.

To create change you will need to start with the proper focus. When we mention focus, we are talking about the energy or vibration you emit toward your new desire. If you look back over your past focused energy, you will see patterns of behavior prior to any major change in your life situation. You may notice that there were periods of time of depression or non-

ॐ

positive energy flow and that was replaced with a more positive flow. This flow behaves similar to water flow; it goes where it meets the least amount of resistance. From this viewpoint, if you are already in one pattern of flow and decide that you want to change, it will take a shift in habit to redirect your heading.

If it is mental flow you want to change, then you will do well to watch it as the observer, prior to deciding what you want to do. When you observe the mental flow, watch how it affects the physical and environmental flow. See how they are interrelated. Retrospectively trace the initial appearance of a previous shift in mental attitude and watch how the physical flow changed. This awareness is imperative if you plan to successfully change any of your creation. It can make creation more interesting, more challenging and more rewarding. The awareness allows you to see how you create your entire life and all of its wonderful rollercoaster rides.

ॐ

17

Drama and the Ego

The only way to know whether or not you are on a path of positive growth experiences is to look at your overall attitude about your life situation. It does not need to be ecstatic or on a perpetual high to feel that you are growing in the way that is most productive. However, the Ego enjoys continuous stimulation. It bores easily.

Think of children and the manner of entertainment they prefer. They want action, change, challenge and immediate gratification. They don't want to be still and hear the inside messages. This is the Egoistic mind asserting itself. It is learning to

ॐ

control the Personality Self and to control others. Even the most passive and quiet child is attempting to control his immediate environment. Many adults use the controlling skills they learned as a child in their adult relationships, as well as in informal interactions. One of the areas of the most intense re-action for the Personality Self is using the child-like skills to control others after you are an adult. People usually are not able to "update" this method of controlling others based on their own maturity level unless they become aware of the chaos it causes.

If people routinely stay in the moment with each interaction, they would not base their action on the needs of the child self, but on the needs of the situation at hand. Imagine your life living in the moment. If a person makes a comment to you, you would listen to the words, sense the energy behind the words and respond to the moment, not the past. You would not be re-active in any manner. You would not need to protect yourself because when you are in the moment, there is no fear of past experiences or future outcomes. You would be able to value each encounter with others all day long, even

ॐ

if you are tired or pressed for time. Your moods would be very stable, i.e., no lows or highs and your personal energy level would be much higher.

Honor simple calm situations because that is what your Soul craves. The Ego plans action in the emotional arena – conflict, tension, change and excitement. Without these experiences it feels nothing. The Ego wants to be stroked or tended to at all times. If the stimulus is not intense enough, it feels nothing. To the Ego, nothing is an extremely uncomfortable state in which to reside. It feels like death - neglected and stagnant.

What about the people who appear to be flat with their emotion? They look at intense situations with confusion and rarely get involved with gossip or promote chaos in an active way. Are these people in the moment? Usually they are not. They live in fear of past and future experiences. Their Ego exerts such control that the walls of protection are up in every direction. The life patterns they see through the Personality Self are too emotional. It is as if they have raw spots all over the walls. They feel that all experiences with others must be controlled or stopped because it is painful. They are in pain the moment they get out of bed. They have low energy because they expend so much energy maintaining and building new walls of protection. When they do not appear emotionally flat, it is because they are using a crutch for support as they peek out or even venture out from the walls of protection. The crutches may manifest in the form of alcohol, drugs or even another person. They will be attracted to people they can live experiences through because they feel that they are either unable or unworthy to live experiences on their own.

If you attempt to say something about the walls to individuals who use this type of protection, they will not be able to understand what you are describing. They have never experienced life in a different manner and can't imagine changing it. They are able to see change in others but find it difficult to apply change to themselves. Do not discount this existence. This behavior serves as an experience on the Earth-level plane. It is similar to a cocoon and can be used as a steppingstone if the individual peeks out over the walls and becomes curious about

ॐ

experiences they are missing. If not, the person is content in his own chaos and resents any formal type of intrusions from others.

You are not here to save others or change the way they feel about the protection of the walls. As you learn to stay in the moment, a person with these walls will either be attracted to the safety of your environment or not. You should not feel obligated to help destroy walls or self-limiting behavior. They must choose to do that on their own. You can provide an environment of non-judgment, peace and unconditional love and that is all. Any change occurring on the part of another comes from within the walls, not from outside them.

ॐ

18

The Ramblings of the Mind

If you think about something perpetually, allowing the thoughts to run through your mind without any type of control, it can consume you especially if the thoughts are centered on a topic of fear, dread or impending doom. By engaging in this habit, you change the true value or the actual effect the situation will make on the Personality Self. Think back to a time this occurred. Did the situation have the same amount of impact you dreaded? Or, more importantly, did the actual occurrence ever come into being at all?

ॐ

The Ego, in an effort to maintain control, takes every opportunity to keep you busy with the past or future. The outcome is very rarely truth. You may even look back and say, "That wasn't so bad after all!" Allowing the mind to ramble and cause emotional body stress is a tremendous waste of energy. It also prevents internal and external observation that is vital to any type of growth. If the mind engages in this type of activity, stop it immediately. Allowing it to go on will create a snowball, increasing the momentum and becoming more difficult to stop.

We recommend that you allow situations to come and go. Source will provide positive learning situations, but you must be "in the moment" to take advantage of the learning potential of any given situation. If your mind is consumed with fear of a situation that is not actually occurring, then a couple of things are forced to happen.

- The current situation cannot be properly handled.

ॐ

- You will miss the beauty of the situation as it is occurring.

The issue you were consumed in was either a past or future thought pattern. Past and future are complete illusions.

You can learn to change this habit of mind rambling. When you first notice it, observe for a moment what the mind is doing and feel the importance or passion the mind places on the activity. Ask your mind or Egoistic Self to stay in the present moment. This is easier to do with a preset or predetermined activity. It can be a substitute thought, a mantra, or a physical movement. You need to break the cycle. Don't criticize the mind - just start your designated activity. A mantra can be thought of as a short prayer. It can be used to call assistance from your Higher Self and as a distraction from the previous mental behavior.

You should be careful not to criticize the habit of mind chatter. It was something you spent years cultivating and perfecting to suit the needs of the Ego. The Ego still exists, so be thoughtful enough to

ॐ

make your goal for this change of habit to be Ego friendly, steering all that wonderful energy into something more productive. You don't want to stop that flow – just redirect it. Channel it into the present moment as much as you can and an entire world of wonderful positive growth experiences will be made known to you.

ॐ

19

What Do You Really Want?

When we talk to you about any of the changes you may want to implement, they are offered as suggestions to make your own life flow better. The changes are not to be used as a judgment against which your motives, actions or thoughts are measured. Be careful not to let these new patterns become actual obstacles. If you find yourself becoming overwhelmed, step back and look at your progress thus far. It is amazing how putting your focus on a few new actions has already changed your awareness.

ॐ

Many people want to know how to become what they see as the perfect person. We want to stress that your focus should be more on what YOU want, rather than what you think you should do or become, based on another's recommendations. If the soft voice inside you is nudging you to accomplish or change something, then that is what you should strive for. Your closest ally is within you. Help make that voice the voice you follow by practicing with it. Ask it to be more obvious to you in a particular way, and if you notice an increase in your understanding, then give thanks to that connection. If you do not notice any new clarity of information, then revisit your request and suggest a new communication tool or trigger. The communication choice should be something easily recognized which will stand out during the routine noise of your day-to-day life.

Take heed to ask for your high level guides and always listen with your heart. If the information is not clear or not coming from a loving place, then stop the communication and center yourself more fully. Ask again.

ॐ

20

Creating a Peaceful Flow

Peace is your nature, your core structure. Peace
and flow are what feel the most natural to your Soul.
Peace does not mean giving in to situations you do
not agree with. It means that you look at the situation
with a new pair of eyes and process what is going on
in a new manner. There may be a difference between
your Soul's desire for the outcome of a situation and
the desire of your Ego. There may be a discrepancy
between the two. Habits from this Earth-level plane
will insist that they are the most important to be
satisfied. Which way feels calm? Which way feels
good, happy and joyful? Which way feels that conflict

ॐ

has been reduced? You will be able to find your answer with your heart.

Your path is not difficult to find when you are willing to be honest with your desires and understand that you may not be ready to find that path yet. Perhaps you want to continue a bit longer on the road you are on. You may be learning valuable lessons in the direction you are going now. You cannot push yourself more than what you are truly ready for. We have noticed that this is difficult for many people to understand. They believe that if they ignore what the Ego wants then it will eventually go away. But these desires have a way of becoming more and more of a distraction as time goes by. The desires develop a life of their own and will one day demand attention.

If you find that you have had difficulty obtaining the flow in your life that you want, it may be because you have not addressed the needs of your Ego.

Watching your own energy and habits will give you wonderful insight about the direction of your path. Find out what you really feel inside. Be sensitive to any negative patterns of behavior you have

ॐ

developed because of external forces. You may be continuing those thought patterns in an effort to protect yourself. Remember that each day is an opportunity to observe yourself and find new ways to gently nudge your path in the most joyful direction.

ॐ

21

Add Comfort to the Body

When one is attempting to comfort or heal the body, it is good to first observe the energy flow to that area. The area with discomfort will have a reduction in energy flow. See where the blockage occurs and attempt to look outwards from inside your body. As you observe the general area, can you see or feel any differences? Are you able to detect any subtle changes in patterns or even in heat flow?

You can influence change to that area by first getting in touch with energy, observe the area you desire to change and then send a vibration to that area.

ॐ

Send Light, color or whatever you are drawn to, and project to that area. Begin with a frequency that will resonate on a small focused area and see if that resonance causes beauty, change in flow, or a change in sensation. Keep playing with it until a tiny shift occurs. Stay with that focus and see if you can intensify or modify the focus you have. Can you expand the area? Did it cause a change in color or flow or even heat or cold? As you practice this, you will become more sensitive to what will cause a shift and what kind of focus you want to project.

You may choose to radiate energy to a particular discomfort someone else is experiencing. Simply include that individual in a focus of energy and set an intention for their highest good.

ॐ

22

Allow Others to Be

Why would a person create a situation that is so uncomfortable that it appears to have no logic or reason? When you ask yourself this question, you need to realize a few things:

- You are unable to see a large enough picture to understand what is really going on.

- You cannot know if the habit or pattern you are observing has already begun to change.

ॐ

What it boils down to is this: do not judge. Do not compare; you need only observe. You cannot help the situation any more than by observing it, and sending Light and Love. The Source will use your Love in the perfect manner to initiate what the next shift might be for that individual. You should not attempt to control how the Love is used. Know in the deepest area of your Being that all is happening for a reason.

If you feel that a situation near you is affecting you in a negative manner, remove yourself from it or change your attitude about it. Your personal perception is the only behavior you truly have control over. Peace will come to you when you are able to accomplish this!

ॐ

23

Are They Really Doing Their Best?

Some people think that if they ignore a situation or emotion that it will dull or go away entirely. Perhaps they think they can wait it out. They hope they will not have to change or want an external shift to occur somewhere else. What they are attempting to do is avoid pain or discomfort, either emotional or physical. This habit is such a consuming force that many people will opt to stay in an unhappy painful relationship or situation rather than assess their options and implement change.

The pain or state of despair appears to drain them of the necessary energy needed to shift

ॐ

consciousness. They appear to be stagnant individuals but in reality they are in a constant state of conflict or stress.

This apparent strife can cause such an uncomfortable state that the person may shift to a more prosperous reality. If not, they can become totally consumed in the victim role and stay there their entire existence.

Living in a state of stress may appear on the surface to be a waste of a functional life, but try to see the individual as a learning tablet, filling pages and pages with present life circumstances. When you see it from this perspective you can see that their Soul is collecting "data," so to speak.

Nothing is wasted at the level of Source. You see, there are no time constraints in this plane. That is why we as guides do not judge or set value on an individual's chosen path. It just is.

You must not judge. You can never "own" enough information to accomplish anything through judgment. Unlearn this habit and your personal happiness will increase tremendously. As you release this habit, you will find a sudden surge of energy,

ॐ

opening up new areas of possibility to experience the Love and Light available to you from Source.

Believe!

ॐ

24

Balance Earth and Soul

The world that you see and feel connected to is a wonderful playground. Do not allow yourself to become so attached to it that you are unable to focus on Truth because of the movement of the masses. Stay sober to the idea that you belong here at this time in the perfect form you already have.

When you feel sad or in any way out of sorts, concentrate on grounding yourself. One way is to connect with the Earth. Feel, touch, smell, and explore the gifts she has to offer. Let her tempt you back into Love with life. When you find balance between the connection with your Soul and the

ॐ

Earth, you will feel the most balanced and productive. You will be able to spread your wings to explore both worlds and find the numerous ways the Earth and Soul compliment and expand the other. One without the other is more of a half-life, causing struggle, unnecessary difficulty and pain. As an individual regains balance, a sense of calm and peace comes. The Earth has so many lessons she can teach you. Be open; listen to the early morning song or the evening stillness. Find the secrets; explore the hidden spaces similar to the way you explore during meditation.

Be present and in the moment when you are outside. Ask for her connection, then feel her reverence for you and return the Love. You will feel a recognizable opening to your Self that is offered only here. She is honored when you recognize the connection you have with her and will come to you with many gifts. Work to combine both worlds so they are in perfect balance - no competition, no forced relationship just simply a pure loving state with no demands on you.

ॐ

25

Become Sensitive to Your Path

The desires that you feel are based in both the Spiritual and Earth-level domains. Both are necessary to experience a fulfilled life. Do not attempt to shut off some of your desires while you focus on others. A better approach is to balance the desires of the Personality Self and the Soul Self. One way to do this is to observe the everyday desires of the Personality Self and decide if they are appropriate to enhance your path in the direction you now desire. The ideal state is to be able to enjoy the pleasures of residing in the human body, but not be consumed by them.

ॐ

To do the balancing act, you can start by listening to input from both the Personality Self and the Soul Self while you are in a quiet state. You will realize that, if you are calm and quiet when you do this, there will be very little conflict. They work together when you give them permission to communicate. They both chose this existence, and will work together quite nicely with practice. As with any relationship, there will be fluid times and there will be times of confusion, but, with conscious effort, peace will be obtained. You cannot do this passively; it must be an active and loving learning process.

As with other new endeavors, you will want to start out slow and be non-judgmental of the perceived success or failures you create.

If you are able to get a glimpse of a partnership between the Personality Self and the Soul Self for any given situation, then consider that situation the path to follow.

You will find that, when there is internal conflict, it is not the time for action. If you do proceed, it will be re-action. As you feel internal conflicts, know that you should do nothing. Wait and listen; be calm and

ॐ

suddenly you will know what your best action should be. Again, this requires that you step out of the external energy or processes going on around you and focus on the inside.

Stepping back and finding the internal rhythm is the action that requires fine-tuning. The information or guidance you receive will always be perfect – it's just difficult to get still and hear it!

This new activity will require a specific process for you to follow. Practice using a trigger to help you become centered or grounded, and then use that process when you are in need of balanced information or advice. It will come. This is not reserved for only a few, but available in abundance to all who search. You will be welcomed with open arms and much celebration from those in the Spiritual plane.

We as guides are able to see the big picture, which is the reason we do not get tangled up in the moment-to-moment decisions you may make. You are loved and appreciated in a way you cannot perceive at this time.

ॐ

Your development of the skills necessary to go inside to ask for guidance is the goal of all of us who work with you. We have many tools at our disposal to assist you and we continually live in a state of non-judgment, love and peaceful flow. This is why we care so much about you and do not feel "put out" by any of the choices you make. We wait, knowing that one-day one situation at a time; our guidance may be useful to you in some way.

ॐ

26

Blend the Personality and Soul Self

Today we would like you to think about the feasibility of acting completely under the direction of your Higher Self.

As you become more aware of your carefully developed habits, you create a state of observation. This observation allows you to slow down and focus on each moment as it is forming. **This focus is the entire secret. The focus is the experience and completion. The focus is the goal of the path.** When you focus, you are able to see how you can blend your Soul Self with your Personality Self. You need not toss out the personality, for it provides the

ॐ

color or texture for the experiences in the Earth-level plane.

When you are able to focus and observe, you continue to be who you were born to be. In those moments you release the need for drama and pain to be the center of each experience. With this awareness, the peace, harmony and bearing of the entire situation is humming with upward flow. The personality is content and fulfilled with this moment. The pearl becomes a deep-seated satisfaction that surrounds the past, present and future, blending them together and producing a state of balanced peace in that moment. The experience lasts longer and longer with practice and the Personality Self eventually learns to crave this new expression, development and actual creation through peace.

Becoming one with the Soul Self is learning to enjoy this plane with a tone that attracts a rich and varied set of experiences. The situations will never become boring because they are each so unique. The tones of the experiences harmonize and create patterns, which amaze even the most experienced individual.

ॐ

The task is not to avoid life, but to shift the focus from one of low-energy cravings to one of amazed radiance for each wondrous experience!

ॐ

27

Broadening the View

Why do many people do things the hard way? It just seems that way because you as an individual are unable to see any situation from a large enough viewpoint. It is also because you are seeing the situation in a completely subjective way. For instance, have you ever listened to a friend or co-worker and *wondered* about their view on the subject at hand? If you have, then be thankful that you were given the gift of vision. You have a different perspective of the situation than they do. Vision will come from a variety of sources. It may be evident all at once or it may come in small increments. That is why, when

ॐ

you mull over an idea or situation, you gain new insight. You are changing your perspective or angle of view. By doing this you are increasing your ability to see a situation objectively.

If your desire is to broaden your vision, invite your Soul Self to assist you. You can do this mentally or out loud, but ask for guidance from your Soul Self and then be still, relax and listen for a response. This, like everything else you learn, takes practice. The response may come as a sudden knowing, as an idea, or even a song you hear. It could be a book title, a comment from someone, a soft voice as you are engaged in an activity.

If you ask others about their ability to see a situation clearly, they will usually tell you about instances of good luck with "sudden awareness of information." When you are aware, information will come to you in many ways. Always be alert to unique patterns of behavior or coincidental comments from others. On the Earth-level plane you should not discount any learning avenue. Experiences can be very enjoyable when perceived this way.

ॐ

28

Become the Stillness

Develop your ability to stay out of mental chatter by setting aside a special time each day to be still. It is best to do this at the same time each day. You don't need to meditate - try sitting quietly or walking in a park. Simply select an activity that slows your mental processes. Because you have been conditioned to keep the mind energy going, stillness may be a challenge to master. Be thankful for just a glimpse of stillness. Any amount of stillness is a wonderful accomplishment! Your goal is to be able to feel/see/experience stillness just long enough that two things occur:

ॐ

- You realize that you can do it!
- It tempts you to do it again!

Your Soul Self will direct you and encourage you to practice. It will be the most natural state you have experienced - and with good reason. It is your true state of Being without input from the Earth-level plane. It will trigger a remembering or curiosity very deep within you.

As you learn to be still, you can learn to listen to your own inner guidance. Ask your Light guides or, perhaps, your Soul Self to be as obvious as possible with you. You must give them permission to work with you. Light guides or Beings of Light and the Soul Self will only offer information based in love, never aggressive or negative thoughts. Even if the subject is about something undesirable, you will be offered enlightenment with loving words or nudges. There is never a true high-level guide or Soul Self that will ask you to do something morally wrong or even questionable. If you feel you are being guided inappropriately, ask that source to leave and stand fast to your desire to have your Soul Self guide you!

ॐ

29

The Choices We Make

To know what you want to experience and how to get there while in the Earth-level plane can be confusing. Your choices or desires are based on what your Personality Self deems to be truth. This perception of truth plays an important part in your ability to select situations for growth, which may or may not be what the Soul Self feels is the most flowing direction to go.

Take, for example, choices made in choosing careers or relationships. If the personality has had negative experiences, it may find a repeat of the situation desirable. There is comfort in what you

ॐ

already know, so even as a choice is made, the choice could be based in fear, familiarity or even the desire for change. A choice based in fear still has the potential to create a learning experience of joy if it is swayed in that direction. For example, fear of being judged may encourage you to "do your homework" thereby producing behavior that brings growth and joy. On the other hand, fear may lead you into an action that brings about more chaos and frustration.

As you design a path of joy and growth, you are able to make more positive choices and remove yourself from a path of experiences that are based in what you have labeled negative learning experiences.

You have the opportunity to make decisions many times a day. If you make your decisions "in the moment," your Soul Self is able to communicate easily with your Personality Self. The ideal process would be to stay aware so that all decisions are based in this realm. You would be surprised how much influence the spiritual plane can be for you, if you ask.

Many people ask for guidance, but they either don't like the answer or they don't trust what they

ॐ

heard. Not to worry, even if the choice is based solely in the desires of the personality, it can still be a wonderful learning experience no matter what the outcome. This is why Spirit is able to offer love, advice and new insight without holding onto the outcome of your decision.

ॐ

30

Creating Balance in Your Life

People use experiences from this existence to process and learn how to use their own Soul attributes for each situation. The Personality and Ego are products of the Earth-level plane and without them it would not be easy to survive. The Ego is not the enemy; it is necessary, useful and can be a beautiful way to enhance your experience here. The difficulty arises when you shut out the Soul Self and all the spiritual guidance available to you and focus entirely on the Ego.

By focusing on one aspect of your life in exclusion of the others, you are thrown out of

ॐ

balance. You are better able to maintain balance in this life by utilizing the resources that are available to you without the need to focus too much on any one method. You don't need to become a monk to be happy.

Most of you would enjoy your life much more if you could balance joy, excitement, pain and fear on a daily basis. You do not need to avoid or attempt to avoid the lessons, but just put less energy into either of the extremes. You do not really need excitement and change, or even control and stability, to be happy. *True happiness comes through passive observance and moment-to-moment clarity in what is going on inside you as well as outside you.*

To learn this process, select a time, perhaps ten minutes or so, and observe all the external stimuli. Feel, see, hear the external stimuli and then shift your awareness to all the internal stimuli - body sounds, feelings, skin sensations, heartbeat, etc. Finally, shift your attention to the thoughts of the Ego. Ego self-talk may be a significant distracter in your life.

ॐ

As you learn about yourself and the external environment, you will learn how to enjoy a balanced state of existence rather than attaching yourself to the extremes of internal or external involvement.

ॐ

31

Helping Others

When you choose an action, you have opened yourself up to an entire realm of possible outcomes. You may have chosen to go in the direction of growth from the view of the Soul or you may have chosen the action based on the desires of the Personality. Either avenue is functional for learning. The Soul views each situation as pure experience, whereas the Egoistic Self sees situations as a path to obtain an emotional experience: thrill, action, drama, excitement or pain and sadness. Yes, the Egoistic Self may choose actions that cause pain because it wants

ॐ

to feel alive. The Ego needs to have stimulation, and negative emotion is filled with power.

Never assume that all people you meet want to be well or healthy. Never assume that a person, who appears to be suffering from lack of material goods, family support, or even food, wants help to change the situation. They may have been "experiencing" just fine prior to your intrusion! That is why, when you work with someone or offer assistance to obtain a goal that your personality views as logical or necessary; the other individual may refuse your advice or help. It is a simple matter, really. You cannot know what the best action for another person truly is. The majority of your energy should be expended to learn the desires of your Soul. By doing this, you automatically attract situations to which your actions of support and love will provide the most benefit. Your ability to "help" others will be less stressful and more focused and productive as you get in touch with the desires of your Soul prior to offering assistance.

It is necessary for individuals, who have chosen professions that focus on educating or helping

ॐ

others, to be thoughtful of those who state they want to change a behavior. They may actually fear change and perceive change as a larger hurdle than the action they say they want to change. These behaviors may be basic life habits, methods of interaction with others, all the way to self-destructive habits such as abusing one's body with drugs, alcohol or staying in a relationship in which they are either emotionally or physically abused.

You must attempt to focus on the truth or energy behind the actions and never judge if that individual goes back to a habit that you feel is destructive. Your only role should be to articulate what you are able to provide with boundaries that are well communicated, and then allow the other individual to choose an action. If a person does not do what you thought was best, you must accept what is and not become emotionally drained because of his or her choices. Simply be still, slow down your emotional re-action and allow the Source to step in. You did your part. You were successful in offering an upward spiral energy that will ripple through the Universe, initiating positive change in the Universe as a whole.

ॐ

We want you to understand the following:

- Your energy directed toward another when that individual comes to you for assistance, is a proper form of offering.

- It is inappropriate to chase after an individual to offer assistance.

- It is unwise to focus on the outcome of the other's action after you have offered the requested service or advice.

ॐ

32

Why Do You Want to Help?

Focus on where the desire to help is coming from. Sometimes the act of assistance is misconstrued to look as if you are offering a service to another, but actually it is a guise to have your own needs met. The choice to help another person and the reasons to do it may be embedded in subconscious and conscious thought processes.

Before you offer support to anyone, it is wise to assess the reason you are offering a service to someone else. Ask for guidance from your Soul Self to assist you in being aware of your true motivation and intention.

ॐ

33

Cultivate Clarity

Clarity comes to those who ask for it. Clarity offers you release from your pain and misunderstandings, which may be based in the actions of others or your own actions. Stop a moment and ask for clarity and it shall be given to you.

Clarity is a great and powerful gateway to personality awareness, as well as spiritual awareness. If you truly want to understand the motive of a given situation, then you should ask at that moment. Clarity is always available to the seeker, but you must not be trapped by the Ego into believing that the resulting

ॐ

action, thoughts, or feeling was "natural" or just happened.

Asking for clarity is a wonderful habit to cultivate and offers many benefits. It will center you because you will need to ground yourself to be aware of a response. It will humble you to receive the information and it will educate you, if you allow it to. Repeating this request regularly creates an open connection with your personal guidance, making it more fluid.

The insights you receive may begin to have patterns of information. You should watch for this. You are being given a gift! You can change or accept motives or causes for your behavior when you see that you consistently have the same guidance. Habits are only behaviors you develop over time. So it stands to reason that over time, with reminders and conscious effort, your acquired habit can be stopped.

Gain practice by requesting clarity for insignificant behaviors you have. This is one of the meanings of the phrase, "you can choose to learn through pain or joy." When you ask for clarity consistently, you are exposed to truth. This will

ॐ

prevent you from investing a significant amount of energy in a situation that may result in long-term or short-term pain. You are given the opportunity to alter your behavior before it generates the energy or vibration that may cause discomfort.

Remember, before this can work, you must be honest with yourself and your guidance and not skew or alter the responses you receive. Have an honest energetic desire to have truth delivered to your heart (not your mind) and you will be exposed to a new sense of Being.

The result will be in the form of flow and joyous experiences in your life. Situations will flow because your actions and thoughts will be in the direction of your chosen upward path. You need not struggle when your thoughts, actions or desires are in accordance with Source.

Realize when you are struggling, that it is time to ask for guidance and it will come with gladness and enthusiasm from your Guides. This is what we want to do for you! This is our mission. It is not an inconvenience for us. We are at your beck and call for this very perfect reason. We want to assist your

ॐ

decisions by giving you the clarity you need to create joyous uplifting and growth-orientated flow.

ॐ

34

Dealing with Issues of Abandonment

L et's look at a life experience that may be called abandonment. To the Egoistic mind, it refers to a situation in which a person is left without the support or protection from the world they feel is necessary. It is an emotional response to a perceived physical withdrawal by another individual, or it can be a response to an emotional withdrawal from another.

Many people allow the Ego to scar the psyche to a point of fearing all forms of separation. This may produce a personality that projects the fear of abandonment into its surroundings, which in turn,

ॐ

will create relationships to mirror that fear back to them.

If this occurs, you must choose to see from the eyes of the Soul Self and stop that pattern from repeating itself. You must see that no matter what the physical conditions around you, you are always part of a greater whole. You can never be alone, for you are as a droplet of moisture in a cloud. You may not see the rest of the cloud, but if you stop and identify with your Higher Self, you will be able to commune with your Spirit.

Abandonment is only perceived on the Earth plane, not in the Spiritual plane. One may actually "die" of not being cared for appropriately: however, that condition is of itself a valuable experience for that individual, still being of value.

One example of this is the grief caused from aloof parents or parents who leave the care of the child to others. If this is something you are in the midst of, practice the skill of becoming one with Source to strengthen your Trust. Through this, you will find freedom.

ॐ

35

Develop Self-Love

Intelligence comes in many forms. Many people are unaware of their own gifts because they are making a comparison to a standard outside of themselves. It becomes difficult to see your own special nature when you were taught as a child that you were unimportant or insignificant. When this type of environment is imposed on children, they will compare themselves to an unattainable standard, no matter what they achieve.

Self-love is achieved when you begin to accept who and what you are and begin to see the value and uniqueness of your own person. Self-

ॐ

love/appreciation is necessary to grow. Avoid becoming an intense critic of yourself. With criticism comes negative emotion and with negative emotion comes stagnation. ***Stagnation is what the Personality Self should be wary of above all other states of mind.***

Stagnation is the heavy price of self-judgment and the inability to see clearly. Your vision is hampered beyond the ability to self-correct, which sometimes initiates the self-destructive behaviors of self-doubt, fear and paralyzing self-criticism. You should focus on the Soul Self to escape this common human habit. The Soul Self forgives, releases, and promotes healthy habits and desires. It will not propagate negative behaviors or thinking patterns.

As you maintain a consistent level of Soul awareness, you become a true temple of Source and learn to see what traits or characteristics should be valued and which ones should be given less thought energy. When an individual's thoughts go to their perceived deficits, then energy will go in that direction making the issue more powerful to you.

ॐ

If you were to change focus, then the wind would be taken from these sails and eventually the previous course would no longer exist. This can be accomplished through diligent effort and persistent awareness in the patterns of your self-talk.

Remove the energy from negative self-talk and the Soul Self will bring in a tremendous amount of energy to guide and nurture you. This becomes self-love or intelligence. The vibrations are the path. When a positive vibration is established, you are in the proper frame of mind to receive any information you choose for growth.

ॐ

36

Reducing the Downward Spiral

Ahhh, the flow of your life, it has its ups and downs. That is what most of you experience. The fluctuations are caused by your state of mind and the connection you nurture. Do you sometimes feel defeated or fearful? Perhaps you experience a down period? These emotional states are not to be feared. During these times it is important to say to yourself "I am having a downward spiral of energy." Look at it. Is it familiar? Does it feel good? Can you find the source or feel the location in your body where heaviness is building up? Is the area that you feel the

ॐ

lack of flow the same area that the lower vibrational energy is coming from?

The more you learn while in this state, the more likely you are able to identify when a low mood is coming. Touch it. Look at it as a child who is observing something for the first time. This is the best place to grow. Be honest with yourself and see if something inside you likes this low feeling.

You are not a failure to find yourself in a downward spiral of thought. The true sign of spiritual growth is identifying what is going on and opening up and asking for uplifting, clearing and harmonizing energies. This may be difficult to do when part of you wants to mentally continue the negative thoughts, while another part wants to step out and observe. Ask for assistance. Stand your ground. Call for assistance as quickly as you can and hang on to a single positive picture or thought as long as you can. You will see the mood lift and the energy around you begin to shift.

While the energy adjusts, take note of your physical environment, such as the colors, textures

ॐ

and even the air temperature. When you stepped out of the negative spiral, did any of that change?

Some people choose to stay in that spiral their entire life or perhaps a major portion of an existence. So, being down a few hours or days is not a reason to feel disappointment. Focus on being grateful for every day that you are focused on your highest good and are offering Love and Light to those around you.

ॐ

37

Judgment Based on Frequency

Judgment: The world as you know it is based on deciding if something you are seeing, doing or thinking about is good or bad, right or wrong, beautiful or ugly, comfortable or uncomfortable, etc. Even as an infant, you learn to manipulate your environment after you have decided your level of comfort. So, realistically, being non-judgmental is really deciding what you are going to "judge" as acceptable and what is not. You probably will not give up judging whether you are comfortable at a certain temperature in a room or whether you want to experience a burn on your hand by placing it in the

ॐ

fire. You even judge what flavor of foods, texture of clothes, or color of items surrounding you that you like. Beauty to you may be ugliness to another.

Rather than deciding to be non-judgmental, perhaps it would behoove you to shift that to sound more like "I choose to see the highest Light in everything I think of." In doing this, you become transparent to the lower energy, which may be perceived as negative.

For example you could look at the person standing on the side of the road, unshaven and dirty, as less of an individual than you, or see him as another expression of the Source. The energy of all forms comes from the Source and a portion of it is vibrating at a perfect frequency in that individual. That path was not the path you chose. But how are you going to determine the appropriateness of the situation you are observing? How do you practice active selection without judgment? You don't. You "practice" becoming one with the Source so that you can resonate or communicate in all situations from a non- Personality Self level.

ॐ

You will always need to choose and discriminate as a personality. With everyone you meet and every experience you have, the Soul Self is able to guide you to see and feel as an individual while still accepting and flowing with the energy that is Source.

ॐ

38

Expanding Your Vision

We would like you to become aware of the manner that we as Guides see the vibrations around us. We see only the frequencies that are emitted at a very high level. We do not see the "solid" objects as you do, but rather the energy that is released. You can learn to see the higher energy that resonates from all beings. You can learn to switch back and forth between your current vision and your "higher" vision.

To initiate higher vision, you will need to center yourself in a way that calms you and enables you to maintain awareness of your connection with your

ॐ

Higher Self. Work with this until you have a sensation of softness of vision. Play with this after your normal time of meditation or other form of connection with your Higher Self. You may notice that your connection will fluctuate, that you will "see" differently from moment-to-moment. That is a wonderful state to be in. Take advantage of this learning state. Play to see the focus you need to increase and decrease your awareness and how you can adjust either your posture or mental state to affect your vision.

Find an object with a large amount of active energy, such as an animal, a person, a plant or a freshly cleaned crystal. Sit and watch the outer edge of the chosen item. Soften your gaze and relax. Call for assistance from your Higher Self. Once you see the slightest difference, concentrate on that for a few minutes then go back to the regular vision you have. Go back and forth for 10 to 15 minutes until you find this easy to do. You are exercising your "shifting mechanism!" After you understand how to do this, you can start with lesser objects such as furniture,

ॐ

cars, etc. It is important to learn what mental state is best for you to maintain the "connection."

Practice in calm situations, then change the outer interferences until you are again challenged, then stay at that level until you master it. This process should be fun for you. Keep your goal of vision as an added bonus in an effort to keep the Ego happy. The Ego likes to learn as long as it feels successful and of value to the emotional body. This process will aid the Ego and the connection with your Higher Self. This is an example of a joint growth project that includes the Ego.

There is a point to remember about the goal of growth. The focus is not on growth away from your Ego and other Earth plane relationships or skills; our goal here is to add another dimension to what you are able to comprehend. This will bring a wealth of information and experience to the current state of your Ego.

ॐ

39

Find the Trigger

You made the decision of where to live to have the lifestyle you wanted. Many of your other choices are not as profound or as glamorous, and yet they still hold a significant influence in the overall tone, pattern and level of enthusiasm you will notice in your day-to-day existence. You must take into account all the smaller decisions and tendencies you manifest.

In an effort to understand what triggers your decisions, find something that enters your thoughts often; sit and reflect on the stimulus that triggers it. Observe the physical re-action to the thought and

ॐ

then play with various actions or thoughts that "null" out that less than favorable response.

The small triggers or thoughts are significant because they are the bases of your growth structure. When you overlook your daily smaller choices or the routine actions, you are doing yourself a disservice. Become the watcher and focus on the mundane to find the true issues you want to redirect. In doing this, you will find release and new awareness or consciousness.

If you find that you avoid scrutiny in a particular area of your life, know that this is the very area that screams for attention. The Soul Self knows where flow is restricted and will attempt to assist you in identifying the cause of the blockage. View these thoughts of introspective analysis as little jewels of Light, being presented to you from above. Look at the initiator of the lack of flow. What does it affect? What made you first aware of the shift from your natural balanced state? Was there a warning sign? Perhaps you got a brief "hit" that something was changing.

ॐ

Choose to perfect this process within yourself by establishing a method that works for you to assist and maintain an upward momentum in your life.

Enjoy!

ॐ

40

Formulation of Thought

This is the first time to discuss the formulation of thought. Thought has many facets and can be confusing to the new student. The basic form of thought is from the Universal Source. It is the energy that connects all Beings and masses. As you have a thought, it is made of a multitude of frequencies with a core or center frequency. As you think, you magnify particular frequencies and diminish others resulting in a very unique vibration.

This extreme variability in creating thought and its resultant vibration is how each of you are One and yet so different. This is the reason each person looks

ॐ

and acts different even though there are billions of people on earth. There are countless combinations of frequencies to choose from, with the added ability to shift as you acquire more experience and your desires change.

It is magical and exciting to see how beautiful the Soul is and how it relates to others in the environment it attracts. The frequencies you emit will determine what comes into your existence and to what degree they will influence you. When things near you resonant with frequencies similar to yours, you are more likely to be influenced by them. If you do not have similar resonance, then you may not notice the existence of the frequencies.

As you are exposed to new frequencies that resonate with you, then your own unique vibration may choose to take on the new frequency. As these experiences add up, your core frequency is modified.

You can choose to release a particular resonant frequency you have outgrown or one that is no longer serving your highest future. By choosing to identify with a new frequency, you can change what resonates with you.

ॐ

As you do this, you will still notice the old frequencies or habits, but you will be able to discard them or even examine them by choice now, rather than be consumed by them. If you are experiencing a thought that resonates at a frequency you do not want, then substitute it with a visual image, mantra, physical motion or other frequency that shifts your attention from it. If you see something that bothers you, you can choose to increase the bothersome resonance, or choose to resonate another frequency at a "higher, louder" rate, so to speak, which will override or interrupt the frequency or situation that you do not appreciate any more.

Remember, when a situation bothers you, or brings you joy, it must already be in your consciousness at some level or you would not even notice it.

As in all of the teachings written here, changing old habits and attitudes as you become aware of them will take practice. Focus on the desired frequency. It is not a matter of force; it is a matter of initiating a new frequency that resonates joy in your current state of consciousness.

ॐ

41

Get the Most Out of This Existence

Your journey is all-encompassing and consuming. The journey is your means of obtaining exactly what you want. You have surrounded yourself with a perfect means of education through observation and experience only available in the Earth-level plane. You knew what you were doing and you are learning to remember your goal. As you remember, you expose yourself to higher frequencies that will create experiences less about drama and more about beauty and joy. The experience of joy triggers more remembering.

ॐ

Your previous training was one of comparison and differences. Now, by focusing on similarities and flow, you can practice becoming an observer. As an observer you will be able to maintain your own state of flow while you send energies of love and acceptance outward toward the rest of humanity.

As you focus on similarities in others or on similarities in the actions of others, you can find the area that is emanating from the Source of Love. The Source of all energy has an amazing cohesion that can be visible to you. Look for it daily in all persons and objects. Practice while you feel a strong connection with your Higher Self and then you will remember to see the energy each time you have a new experience.

Practice! Practice! Practice!

ॐ

42

Growing Too Fast

One way to know if you are moving toward your goal of spiritual awareness is to have a point of measure for yourself. Develop a baseline or benchmark so that you can go back and see how much you have changed your thinking. One way to do this is to keep a diary of some thoughts and feelings about various topics, so that you can remember how you functioned then compared to now.

Over time this benchmark will change and show you how much you have grown by pointing out specifics rather than just the general thoughts you

ॐ

may develop. The general concepts can get lost in the background noise of your Earth-level life, but the specific instances will jog your memory and give you immediate feedback to work with. You will be amazed how particular situations bothered you or how previously you were caught up in someone else's issues. Now you can't even remember your previous pathway because you feel so comfortable on this path.

By keeping the notes, you will also be able to use them to motivate yourself to continue with your current routine. If you see significant change you may decide to purposely focus on another new path for yourself. By looking back, you can watch your progress and decide what you want to call significant shifts and what you want to call regrouping time.

You need to grant yourself time in which you do not feel the urge to push yourself for growth. It is valuable to take breaks so that you can re-examine, rest and assimilate what you have been working on. It is a form of recharging and motivating yourself by understanding that these are the times you bring the new energies to your core and make them part of

ॐ

you. From there you develop a stronger base, giving yourself a new vantage point from which to grow.

It is important to grow at a rate that is comfortable for you. One way to check your comfort is to see if you are able to engage in your Earth-level life without feeling disoriented or disconnected. If that does occur, you need to slow down and just be. Become an observer, a watcher and think about what is being done. Be mindful to cultivate the joy of dwelling in the Earth plane; working, loving and playing at the same time that you are growing your awareness as a Spiritual Being. It is not a process that should exclude daily life, but rather it should value existence and growth in both areas of your life.

ॐ

43

Healthy Connection

One of the most growth-oriented ways to look at life on the Earth-level plane is to think of yourself as an observer not a player. If you come from this perspective, you are less likely to become engrossed in the day-to-day stresses. You will be less likely to carry stress and tension in your body muscles or get headaches. This process will reduce emotional attachment to issues that may cause grief, sadness and the feeling of being overwhelmed. Observers do not ignore or deflect the emotional content of any given situation; they can empathize and support the players, but they do not become entangled in the massive threads that are desperately attempting to attach themselves to anyone in the vicinity.

An observer allows emotion to be present without attaching a judgment of worth. From this state there is no reason to place any value on the occurrence, the emotion just is, and will pass through in seconds unless there is deep resistance to it. In this way, the observer is able to maintain a neutral and flowing mental state, which increases the connection with Spirit.

To do this, you will need to consciously focus on **not** being what you are thinking or doing. You can use a statement such as "I am only an observer or I am not the cause of _____, I am an observer." This may assist you in clearing your vision. Clarity is another means of maintaining your focus and seeing truth at all times. This will aid with observing life, too. If you are able to maintain clarity, you will be able to reduce the desire to force outcomes in any given situation, thereby creating flow in yourself.

The state of flow is one of the highest states to maintain and provides a platform for one to connect with both the Spiritual and Earth planes. From this

ॐ

platform you are able to provide a wonderful quality of support and love to those in your life.

ॐ

44

How Do I Love?

There is only one way to love, to truly love, and that is from the center of your Being. Most people use a filter created by the Ego and apply it to the Personality Self's actions and judgments. This filter determines who you will love, how you will love and who you will allow to love you. This behavior of filtering does not come from your state of Being. This type of monitoring interferes with the satisfaction that you desire in your life.

Most people feel they love exactly the way they should, but if this were true, there would be no pain, deceit or hatred. Why do you think if things were

ॐ

different the pain or issues would not be there? Actually, until you connect with the Soul or Higher Self, the patterns you have in your life will continue. Each circumstance will be ripe with lessons and examples for you to simply observe. Be still and ask each day, "How can I love myself more? How can I express my love to Source more readily? How can I love others more thoroughly?" All the questions have the same answer. Feel the love of the Source through your heart center where it is unfiltered, pure and full of Light. When you feel the Love of the Source, you are able to feel the same love from others.

Do not fear this. You can feel through this center with complete abandon. You are protected, loved and nourished from this center. We are all here to protect you and honor your requests of Love and Light.

Be brave. Let go and know that all is Love and you are a bright Light to so many others who need your guidance and support. You cannot fail; the Light matches your abilities to your desires.

Trusting the power of the Source is an obtainable quest for most of you. To apply the same trust and

ॐ

non-judgment to relationships that contain Egoistic dreams and patterns is the challenge. It is a continuum. Start today and change the Light of your Being and bring more light into the world!

You are Love

You are Peace

You are Eternal.

ॐ

45

Positive Creative Nature

Today you will need to think of ways you might best manage the perceived time and space that you find yourself in. This would be a form of visualization to create the environment and situations around you. You could think of it as creating form and Light around yourself. In reality you already do this with great consistency. Because your conscious mind is not in control, you feel that you are not successful.

Your judgment of success or failure is based on an erroneous measuring or comparative system. The fact is that you are a continual creator. The point of

ॐ

your focus may be all that needs adjustment. Currently, most of you have great difficulty maintaining a point of focus that is able to bring the outcomes you desire. You can shift your focus by first determining what it is that you want, then, observe as you step away from that creative point either in thought, words or actions. You will surprise yourself with the amount of time you spend focusing either in the opposite direction of your desire or off of center in many directions.

The problem is not your creative ability. It is that your point of interest keeps changing, which makes it difficult to build up enough momentum in the direction you "wish" for. Time is momentum. Spend more time creating - thoughts, words and actions - toward your desire and less time in thoughts, words and actions about what you do not want to create.

You could take paper and pen with you and make a mark on the paper each time you leave focus. This will help you be aware of the chronic nature of your habit to sway from the target you want.

Give no thought energy to anything that is not in complete alignment with what you want created.

ॐ

Your connection with Source is always at your beck and call, even if you think no one is paying any attention to you. The energy is what creates, the energy of thoughts. There are no Beings sitting in another place listening to your wishes and deciding which ones are valuable or worthy of creation. You are the creator, you are the stimulating force, and we are here to help you remember this.

ॐ

46

It's About the Effort Involved

What many people want is a means to maintain a lifestyle on the Earth that allows them freedom with as little effort as possible. If an individual is given all wishes without the need to make an effort, the life reality becomes boring. If one lives in this manner, one may lose focus, reason and passion. The desires, passions and even the reason for existing as a Being are based in the process of learning how to create.

You can learn how to enlist the assistance of the Universal flow to produce what you want. The learning includes experiences of lack, becoming

ॐ

aware of desire and then creating abundance. You cannot learn the process if you are always catered to. You must experience it for yourself. For example, art is created in this manner. One feels the lack or desire that is to be filled or expressed through paint, pen, music or movement. The thoughts, planning and execution all entail connection, modification, practice and finally an outcome that fills the void.

A relationship follows the same basic path and offers ample opportunity to modify behavior and situations minute to minute to create flow as an outcome. Growth for the average individual rarely comes to one who is comfortable. Even curiosity contains an amount of discomfort in the moment that encourages you to look around. When you are "wishing" your life was better, think about the wonderful opportunity you now have. Don't focus on the negative or what you wish were different.

Give thanks that you are able to step out of the life drama long enough to desire change and then create what you want by changing the situational resonance to match your new goals. *Remember, you created everything in your life one way or*

ॐ

another. You were not a "failure" when you created your troubles; it is just that now you no longer desire to maintain a connection with them. Once this awareness is achieved, a new set of circumstances will be created. Nothing is given to you on a silver platter, unless you have previously set the energy and done the work to receive it.

The Earth plane is neither a place of constant joy or pain. It is a neutral location that is used as a field of unlimited experience.

ॐ

47

Keep the Flow

Think of a time when you were able to connect with the All-That-Is. A time when your life flowed and things were easy for you. This flow could have been for hours, days or even longer. When you are remembering that time, you are able to re-create that same energy. You can create that flow in your life with only the thought of it. This is of great value to you to use in all situations, good and not so good. Practicing this when you are not stressed is the best way to strengthen the tie to that part of you. Make it a daily habit to find that space inside of you and play with it. This should be a joyful time, full of gratitude

ॐ

and awe at the ability of the Source to help you remember your power.

Would you like to stay in a place of extreme bliss? This is a possibility for you. It is a matter of staying connected to both "Heaven and Earth" or the state of ultimate balance. You can function at a much higher level and reduce the amount of pain you choose to experience. The main roadblock you have is the Ego's desire to maintain the status quo. The Ego wants to maintain its sense of identification, its sense of self, and is bored when situations are going too smoothly. It likes chaos because it feels great energy from the chaos. To the Ego, flow is similar to death because of the level of energy flowing through you, rather than boiling inside and around you.

Keep your physical body centers open to flow, by visualizing the centers as a funnel. Imagine the larger section away from your core and the smaller point close to your spine. When the centers are flowing equally, then you are able to feel bliss! In this state you can take any of the surrounding energy offered to you and filter it through your heart center. As you do this, the energy is able to be modified to a higher

ॐ

frequency and sent out to be used by others. It is beneficial to do this because it raises your own energy pattern. You can practice this when you are exposed to mild or to moderate lower energy. Open your centers, breathe deeply and project the energy you are feeling up and out your heart center. It is beneficial to do this activity when you are feeling down or in a less than positive mood.

🕉

48

Change the Turmoil

There was once a man who lived in a state of turmoil. He was unaware that this state existed in him and assumed that the problem was all around him. It never occurred to him that he was producing the situations and the circumstances that were around him day after day.

One day he noticed a woman sitting by the town well who was obviously not physically healthy, but was smiling about something he was unable to see. He asked her what she was happy about and she said that she was enjoying the feeling of the warm sun on her face. She said that she found that if she enjoyed

ॐ

the small blessings in her life, that more blessings came her way. She said she liked the small blessings better than the physical pain.

This made him think of his turmoil and how perhaps, if he focused on the small blessings, that more blessings would come his way.

By entering this one thought into his head this man changed his entire life experience.

ॐ

49

Knowledge at Your Fingertips

You are blessed with the knowledge of the Source. Your base of knowledge is not limited to your own personal experiences. You have at your disposal all knowledge, all experiences of the past and future. You have the ability to access this entire body of information.

Now your question is, if this is true, then why am I not aware of all this knowledge? Why do I feel that I have significant restrictions on what I know? The answer is not easily grasped. The Universal knowledge base is housed in all Beings. Some Beings are actively engaged with parts or sections of the

ॐ

information, and other Beings are functioning with other sections of the information. One may be more versed in a particular area at a certain time than another, but any concept or thought or even a future motion is in the All-That-Is. Nothing can be fulfilled without it having been in the flow or the Light. When you are in the flow, you can tap into this body of information and request answers, new ideas or new situations to occur.

It, like other topics we have discussed, is more easily accomplished with practice. You need to get still and listen after you present your question. The answer will come to you in the form of words, pictures, feelings or simply a knowing. You may receive the information from another person or even an animal. You see, the Source is in all things. The way the answer comes to you may be in a form that is most familiar with the answer. It may come to you in a form you do not recognize or it may come in a dream. Your task is to open yourself up to receive the information without a preconceived notion of the manner in which it will come.

ॐ

Each time you ask to access the bank of Universal knowledge, your motive, state of Being and the urgency of the matter will influence the outcome. When you make the request, you set energy into motion. The intensity of the energy you project plays a part in the manner you attract the information back to yourself.

You may find that you asked for information, but deep down inside you either already knew the answer or you really do not want to know the answer. Be thoughtful and sincere when you are requesting information. Ask the question as clearly as possible. Do not combine questions together. As you take time to formulate your thoughts, examine your motives, find the true source of the question, and then think about the response.

Perhaps when you look at a question, and prepare to present it to Source, you realize that it has a tremendous amount of low energy attached to it. Questions with lower frequency vibrations are going to travel only short distances and travel very slowly. Questions with high frequencies coming from your heart center are most easily returned to you in a form

ॐ

that is less chaotic and more fluid. Practice sending out your questions and take the time to see if you are housing the answer inside. You will feel the connection to the endless supply of guidance that is yours to enjoy.

🕉

50

Life as an Illusion

You hear and see many things that are embedded in a chronic state of illusion. Even most of the feelings you have are the result of years of conditioning by the Egoic mind.

The difficulty lies in filtering out what is real and what is not real, what is truth and what is not. Many people are unable to even glimpse reality and may deny the very existence of a different reality. Their reality comes from years of experiences piling up, thereby creating a false sense of safety and existence.

In this reality, people have life cravings so intense that they are unable to ignore them. They may think

ॐ

that they should fill the craving/void with more Earth-level challenges or rewards because that is the reality they have created. Actually, the craving is initiated at the Soul level in an attempt to create an awareness of the higher state of consciousness.

Without this internal craving, most individuals would maintain the complete illusion that the Earth-level play is the only existence possible and become impassionate about life. The cravings awaken the curiosity and passion to find more depth to the Earth-level life though the awareness of the Soul Self.

ॐ

51

What Went Wrong?

Sometimes with your desire to accomplish a task, you meet failure. This occurs when the intent was not in alignment with your path or the path of the other individual or individuals involved. Do not be discouraged, but simply put your full attention on the current moment. Don't allow yourself to become stuck thinking about the outcome. Just be.

You may want to think of it in the following manner; each action has the potential to produce the outcome you desire. Your goal would be more easily met if you spent more effort being still to decide what actions are truly necessary for the good of all

ॐ

involved. This would reduce the number of situations that are disappointing. If you are able to hear or sense what actions are appropriate, you are using your natural self for its highest good.

ॐ

52

Listen to Your Thoughts

Listen to the thoughts you hear running over and over inside your head. Allow them to flow without restriction for a while until you find yourself comfortable with them.

Don't try to turn any of the thoughts off or redirect them in any way. Observe and accept them with an opened heart, one of kindness and understanding. You are privy to hearing the most private memories, fears, joys and ideas from the deepest most secret areas you have. Do not chase any thought away because you feel it is not worthy of

ॐ

you. Sit with your entire self for a while without the distraction of any of your routine activities.

Bless any road your thoughts take and help them feel accepted. It may be their first time out in the light, so to speak. The more you do this, the more readily the quiet and shy or fearful thoughts will expose themselves. What are the thoughts most likely to hide in the corner? Did you know they existed? Are you able to hear them out without difficulty? If not, why? Are you afraid to listen to them for fear you might allow them to dominate you? If you listen with the proper intention - the intention to get to know the part of you crying out for truth, crying out for acknowledgment - then you will not be absorbed by that which you have pushed away for so long.

This is a journey of healing, a journey of growth, not one of regression. You are the one who is able to find what weakens you. You can find the root of any perceived weakness if you are honest, still and very attentive. Become the lover of the soft-spoken whispers from the deep area inside of you. Offer them comfort, understanding, physical ease, acknowledgement and patience. Help these root

ॐ

thoughts find their rightful place with all the other thoughts and actions, which are also responsible in their own way for adding to the wonder of this experience here on Earth. Pull them into your heart away from the pit of your stomach. Find each one, each time it peeks out. As you do this, it becomes one of the most beneficial processes for your total health.

Become a Being of total self-love. Love the person you are today. You are the reason life exists. *You are Source made manifest in form - all of you, not just part of you - not just the part of you that you approve of.*

ॐ

53

Personal Growth

Do you know how you are able to complete a growth cycle? A growth cycle is a period of time you spend working on a particular experience. This will overlap with other experiences but if you could separate them, it would be one cycle. During that time, you experience a gamut of feelings, desires and perceived needs. When this occurs, you have more opportunity to connect with your Soul Self and observe the experience from a larger or fuller perspective. The span of time for a cycle is variable, but it needs to be long enough for each experience to be completed. Some exposures take only a moment

ॐ

before a realization occurs, while other cycles may take several lifetimes before you glean the true meaning.

Imagine this: if an experience you are having takes several lifetimes to experience, how can your Personality Self decide which experiences are necessary? How can the Personality Self, without assistance from the Source, determine the value or necessity of any given situation? It cannot. In each case, you must be extremely careful not to decide what an acceptable outcome is or even judge if a particular situation was "necessary."

In the example of war or an activity of global significance, could it be that the mass consciousness is going through a mass realization or growth cycle? Why would a group "path" be any less of an option than an individual path? Now, that is not to say that in this situation you are supposed to fight, you may fight, or demonstrate against war, or even ignore it. If you are able to detach from the Earth life horror of such choices and observe the energy, and actual varieties of group consciousness exposed to such an incidence, you could choose to see the goodness.

ॐ

You could witness groups of people having a common cause and assignments, seeing firsthand the outcome of choices made by fellow soldiers, administrators and even by the local people.

If you are able to stay in the moment, you could see how the human spirit is able to maintain balance even in chaos. You may observe/experience confusion, fear and dread or see miracles of compassion, incredible stamina and forethought. You see, every experience has the opportunity to teach an entire array of lessons. Make your goal to "see" as much as possible from all experiences. Don't assume that because something is painful or negative you cannot learn something. Don't assume you were not supposed to find yourself in that position. Don't judge the value that any situation has to offer to your Spiritual path.

If a particular experience spans a few lifetimes on the Earth-level plane, you are unable to know that. Value is very difficult for you to determine, so it is best if you do what we have been recommending; observe without judgment, do not place blame, do not assume that a situation should be avoided.

ॐ

Trust that your highest good is always in the plan, even on a global level. You are never ever alone without guidance. Learn to feel the guidance in quiet, calm times, so that when things seem out of control you will be able to tap into the great reserve of support, guidance and love available to you.

ॐ

54

Reasoning and Change

Humans believe that their ability to reason and learn from their mistakes sets them above the state of animals, minerals and plants. Actually, it is much more complicated than that. It is more individual. Because of this individuality there is not one set rule for all of mankind as there is for the mineral and plant kingdom. Each person has a set of rules built with the aid of family and friends, which determines how any given situation will be handled.

You may notice in yourself for instance, that the manner in which you interpret a situation changes as you engage in more experiences. As you age in this

ॐ

lifetime, you may change your viewpoint 180 degrees on particular issues! Some people initiate change through a form of reasoning, but actually the culprit of change occurs at the level of the Soul. Think of a Soul as a grain of sand in a clam (inside your Being) and rather than producing a pearl, it initiates change in behavior. It does not dictate the behavior it desires, it simply keeps nudging until the Personality Self becomes uncomfortable or becomes curious enough to pursue a different avenue.

Without the Soul Self, acting in a sometimes-antagonistic manner, humans would simply maintain a comfortable environment or situation once they obtained it. The insights from both the Soul Self and Spirit assist Source in movement forward. The world of Spirit provides inspiration for many new ideas or concepts. For example, this writing is from that plane of existence.

Growth can be observed in many forms. A simple experience may cause someone to suddenly change an entire paradigm of thought. From the limited viewpoint of the Personality Self, change may occur because of low frequency energy found in hatred or

ॐ

murder. These actions cause a large ripple of results at many levels simultaneously. All produce growth or awareness. Awareness will shock a system into a new realization as in injury or fear, or excite a system into a new conscious awareness such as love, joy or peacefulness. The opportunities for change are endless but many are overlooked by the Personality Self unless they are jolted by significant positive or negative experiences.

If one is able to step back and observe - watch, feel, and absorb a situation with the intent to experience it fully - the better the chance growth will take place in a more consistent manner.

ॐ

55

What is Faith?

Faith is the ability to totally believe. To have faith is to be consumed with the passion of love. Faith is to trust that which you know deep down inside to be truth. Faith is to understand from the level of each molecule that there is no such a thing as control in life situations by the Personality Self.

The Universal Power or Source provides the only sense of direction and love you truly need. When things don't go as planned, perhaps it was that the plan of the Personality Self differed from the Soul Self. How do you really know that a Universal goal or outcome is not just over the horizon? How can you

ॐ

angst over something you cannot see or know as truth? Be patient, you must listen and most of all, observe. If you can do this, you will be shown many things all at once from various viewpoints.

With Faith comes a peace-filled life and if that is your desire it is a noble goal, a righteous one indeed. Do you comprehend the significance of this desire? You will take Peace into every situation and see through the eyes of your Soul. All of life becomes clearer and you can actually experience the sensation of impassioned Love for all, not just the people or situations your Personality Self deems worthy of your favor. To be at Peace with the world means to be able to go through each day without the need to control outcomes or have fixed ideas about the path. Faith steps in when you feel weak and gives you strength to continue.

Faith and a peaceful life work hand in hand.

ॐ

56

Resonate With the Essence

There is an essence to all matter. Human nature feels that it can control, or in the very least, influence that essence. The basic energy pattern of essence cannot be stopped. It will always flow regardless of the influences around it. That is its nature, to flow, to continue. That is its beauty, its Grace and its presence. We are all under its influence; we came from it and will return to it. We are going to take our new experiences back to Source one day.

The essence is what drives people to wonder, to question, to yearn and feel alive at any given moment. Only those who have chosen to block out this music

ॐ

are focused on the non-existence. They do not see the flowers in the way they can be seen through and through. They do not see the realness behind the artistic movement or the perfection in all stages of the aging body.

You who read this are making a choice to listen to the essence within yourself and within your surroundings. It can be a special, wonderful experience to look at something or listen intently and FIND the essence. Find the All-That-Is in what you are observing. Can you resonate with it? Now find something that does not appear to have a pure connection with its essence. Can you resonate with that also? The only difference is your focus. Keep shifting until you can join in the joy of that particular expression of the perfection of life.

All of life shifts because it is energy, and energy is never stagnant. Those who look at the movement will never be bored or feel that life has passed them by. They are able to see the movement and go with it, never allowing the mind to feel as though things pass it by. The mind is suddenly part of that flow. It

ॐ

becomes happy, peaceful and content to experience here and now and enjoy all that is given.

ॐ

57

Where Did the Flow Go?

When you attempt to force something to occur, you are not acting out of your Higher Self. Actions or desires in the Earth-level plane need not be fraught with stress and chaos. They can flow. If you feel that flow has been interrupted with any activity, then you may want to practice the habit of questioning the behavior or action you are taking. Ask yourself about the direction you are moving. What is the desired outcome? Is this the only way to obtain it? Are you acting on impulse or an old habit? Are you in the present at this very moment?

ॐ

When you respond to a situation with a sudden impulse, you may find flow, but if you do not, you should stop and think about what is motivating you. Feel what is going on inside your body. Breathe deeply and think about the force behind your desire. Is this for something you want to promote in yourself or in the situation? Does it "feel" right and if not, what feeling are you engaged in? What is your mind doing with the situation? Is it running around defending itself with thoughts of the need to protect or defend? Is it justifying your position? Perhaps it is stunned and wondering why this is happening.

When you become one with your path you will cultivate the habit of listening to your voice. Go deeper and ask, "Will this action create flow in my life?" If your situation involves another person and the manner in which that person responded to you, then you can learn to turn your emotional re-action or physical re-action, into an in-the-moment action.

Ask yourself a question when you notice that the flow of a situation has changed. Ask, "What changed inside me?" "Why did it change?" "What would encourage the flow to return?" "Is timing in the situation important or can a response wait?" "Must an action really be taken now?"

This may be applied to purchases, conversations or any movement on your part. You must remember that you are a co-creator of everything that occurs around you. You are a creature made from Source matter or essence. You have the gift to use that power to the best of your ability; however, to do that you need to identify when you are creating something that is not flowing for you or that will not flow later.

You can manifest whatever you choose.

ॐ

58

What is the Pull of the Future?

Most of you are extremely curious about what is in your future or the future of others. The future draws or pulls humans because the future is what they are taught to focus on even as children. The pull toward the future is an attempt to change what you are experiencing or to enhance your current experience. The present moment is just simply never enough - not enough sensation or movement - but the future will always have more because your Ego taunts you with the possibilities.

Where you are now is exactly where you are! It is the perfect place to be. You created the flow that

ॐ

brought you to this exact spot with all of its little nuances. If you feel that you created a flow that you no longer appreciate, then you can simply nudge the flow in the direction you want.

The future can become a source of disappointment and frustration because it never actually comes. The only reality is this very moment. This moment is your reality. You can experience it as a pleasurable experience or as mundane.

When a person has limited understanding of the concept of being in this moment and is always waiting for the future to occur, depression may set in. The individual becomes either fearful of the change that the future holds or they become lethargic about perceived options. Rather than focusing on the now, the individual may decide the future is the enemy or not to be trusted. By engaging in the habit of focusing on the future, you lose the ability to create positive change in your life.

To truly enjoy or appreciate this existence, one must break the addiction of running toward a new experience and instead, sit and fill the present moment with appreciation and awe. This shift in

ॐ

perspective will then attract more moments full of wonder and ease to fill your every desire.

ॐ

59

Selecting the Experience

The only way to really know what you need to experience is to focus on what is going on with you right now. Look at the situations you find yourself in and how you react to them. As you become aware of your surroundings without judgment, you have a true path to see your past, present and future direction.

Look at your situation in a state of total acceptance and innocence. Use the same state of mind to do this activity as when you are staring off into space.

The path is never hidden from anyone, it's just that many individuals either shut out the information

ॐ

or taint the path. This habit makes the path appear to be an individual occurrence rather than a succession of actions and re-actions.

If you are serious about seeing your path or how the experiences you are cultivating fit into your thought desires, align them and look for the patterns. This way you can see the Ego and how it demands a piece of the action. Write out a variety of re-actions to past or present situations and see how each one makes you feel. The less chaotic, less stressful and calm action will help place you back on a spiritual path.

If you bulldog through life without examining your actions, you cannot expect to be an active participant in directing your own play here in a joy-filled direction. Your life doesn't happen to you, you happen to life, and how you perceive it is a major influence over what you attract next.

If you feel that you are in a rut, look for a new inspiring activity that brings your focus back to your Soul.

ॐ

60

Why Did I Do That?

When many people focus on personal growth, they strive to "become better." They may not understand how to focus on their desire or to even how to define that desire. Your personal growth can mean becoming aware of what and why you do the things you do. You may want to understand why you say the things you say and think the things you think. What is the secret behind who I am? Why do I feel compelled to be angry, sad, depressed, happy, joyful, etc., under particular circumstances?

This knowledge allows you to grow yourself, as it were, and to understand when your connection with

ॐ

Source is in the background or foreground of your thoughts. If your desire is to maintain a strong connection with your Source, then choose the actions, thoughts and feelings that promote feeling good. *Know this truth: your connection with your Higher Self is always steady; it is your awareness of that connection that wavers. While you are in a state of feeling good, you are able to grow yourself in a positive direction.*

If you find yourself in a situation that does not make you feel good, then do not fall into the habit of judging yourself as being weak. All experiences are of value to you, but the trick is to cultivate the habit of non-judgment, so that you do not sink into a more negative state of feeling about yourself.

One method of working to develop non-judgment about a situation is to pretend that you are sitting outside of yourself in a different environment than where you are. See yourself and look for the connection as it truly is, despite your Ego's choice to see only the difficulty or feel the negative feelings. When you sit outside, you will have an opportunity to

🕉

see, with the non-judgment of your Higher Self, what is going on and how to best handle the situation.

You can slow down time so that you can better grasp the meaning and decide what you want to do. Practice will make this become second nature. Ask your guides to assist you with this. They will joyfully do this and be grateful that you trusted them to assist you.

Your guides can help you to stay focused on what you would like to produce in your lifetime. Give yourself permission to sway slightly from your goals. When a negative situation or re-action happens, you are acquiring more information for future experiences and this new situation adds to your mass of knowledge for future events.

As you practice non-judgment of yourself, you become less likely to judge the actions of others. Think about this: *if you have difficulty understanding why you are re-acting to a particular situation, then how can you understand why another person is re-acting a particular way to their situation?*

ॐ

You can create your own inner peace by remembering the connection to your Higher Self. Allow the current situation to take a back seat to the connection you have so that you can focus on actions that bring the joy that you desire.

ॐ

61

Stay in the Moment

When you keep your attention in the moment, you are able to see that walls of fear and doubt are an illusion. If you do this even for an instant, you would be able to see that you didn't need them to begin with. You keep and maintain the walls because of your emotional belief system. This system of belief tells you to protect yourself. But you must ask why? What are you protecting? And then ask whom are you protecting the "what" from?

This perpetual need of self-protection causes you to stay "out of the moment." You probably don't even remember your existence in the here and now

ॐ

without the need to use the walls of protection. Fear is the reason you build the walls, fear of feeling pain or having an experience you decided was negative and not to be repeated again. This becomes a shallow way of thinking. You are judging what the needs of your future self are, based on past experiences.

How do you change this habit of hiding behind the false walls of protection? You do it one minute at a time. Each time you connect with the Source, you step out of the existing play here on Earth and into the true state of the Soul. Using walls of protection came from your training as a child and feels natural. This comfort is an illusion because, with the walls of protection, "flow" is reduced and emotion builds up behind the walls. This emotional energy boils, circles and builds, adding to existing walls and designing or creating new ones.

As you reduce or even eliminate your "walls," you will be able to stay in the moment and maintain a more comfortable flow. You are also able to see current situations without illusion or false features. As you learn to do this your sensitivity to the

ॐ

vibrations from Source is increased. This becomes your natural state.

Staying in the moment releases a tremendous amount of energy that would have been used to maintain the walls of protection. This increase in energy can be seen or experienced by yourself or others as vibration, Aura, Light body!

ॐ

62

The False Belief System

When you think of grief, how do you describe its character? Do you describe it as difficulty, pain, fear and general foreboding? Do you feel that grief is an experience to avoid at all cost?

Grief is a state of mind created because the Personality Self feels that it has lost control, lost control of the future and of the perceived ability to influence situations around you.

When you look at life, in the Earth-level plane, you have absolute control over very little. In essence, the Ego produces a large-scale falsehood of control, which serves to provide a platform for all of your

ॐ

activities. This platform is built on a large number of falsehoods, and if a core section of the structure is challenged, other beliefs rush over to help support the platform that may cause the entire structure to wobble or tilt. This may cause a feeling that the entire world is crashing down.

All of this occurs because you choose to build your belief system on false information, desires and tendencies. When the foundation is shaky or lopsided, you will have much more difficulty maintaining a life of joy or peace. Chaos will always be at the core of this type of life.

Begin rebuilding your foundation. Look at what fears you have. Look at each one and see if it is based in safe secure love or fear-based loss? You will know deep down if a belief is truth or falsehood. How does it make you feel? Do you feel strong and joyful when you ponder on the source of it?

Take any fear you find and expose it. Find the truth that can replace each fear thought and see how you feel with the new beliefs. When you replace the old feelings as they pop up with the newly acquired thoughts of truth, you will find your foundation

ॐ

changing and the opportunities for learning through grief being replaced with lessons learned through joy.

Grief comes from reliance on objects, people or situations based solely in the Earth-level plane. Joy comes from developing a maze of beliefs out of the Universal truth that supports and nurtures you. Strengthen the connection, feel the blessed presence of Source. That knowing becomes the comfort and support you deserve and crave.

Joy, Joy, Joy.

ॐ

63

The Fluid Nature of Things

We would like to teach you another means of focus which may help increase your ability to stay in a higher space or vibration.

Select an object for this experiment. While looking at the object ask the following questions. What are you really seeing? Is it a hard object or a soft object? What type of values do you have for it? When was the first time you remember seeing this item? Does this item bring you good, bad or neutral feelings?

You have an attachment to every object in your environment and you are constantly changing that

ॐ

interpretation. Your analysis of everything in your life is fluid. This is because you are constantly judging your surroundings as either worthy or not worthy. Your mind wants to feel valuable and will create busy-work by making judgments. Use this as an opportunity to see the pattern of the values you place on items and watch to see if the judgments are positive or negative. You can learn a lot about your Ego with this simple exercise. It will reveal your typical nature.

As you experience a negative mood remember to play this game. You may find that the same object you observed at an earlier time has changed to hold a different meaning to you.

Until you feel neutral about all of your judgments, you will continue to need to observe. When you are able to watch yourself and your world with neutrality, you will know you have grown to a higher state of awareness. Residing in this newer state will buffer the times you fall back into the habit of non-neutrality.

Step by step, you will feel more comfortable with yourself and the choices your Ego makes. This

ॐ

process will assist you to better understand why the Ego makes the choices it makes.

Be kind, gentle and patient about your progress, for it is the perfect growth for you. If you push yourself too hard, you will become overwhelmed and lose focus on the creation of a joy-filled life.

ॐ

64

Where Are You in Your Growth?

We want to talk to you about the way you interpret your own strengths and weaknesses. Most of you still use the measuring tools given to you by your parents and the other significant people in your life when you were young. These measuring tools are now outdated. If you continue to use an outdated scale to measure yourself against, then you are creating stress or setting yourself up for failure.

Your old values and desires of what you want to do to develop a satisfied Self are more than likely of little functional use to you anymore. It is necessary to

ॐ

continually change how you measure your success or maturation, based on where you are in your life.

Think of the various individuals who taught you how to make decisions and how to think about what you were doing. When you look back at these individuals do they exude the joy and love you wish to emulate? Do your current desires ring true with what you were shown by example and what you were told as a young one? Perhaps it is time to sit down and formally decide what behavior, thoughts and expression of your Self you want to promote and what you would like to put less energy into.

Write out typical re-actions you have in various situations. Then write next to this how you would prefer to respond in the same situation. Seeing it in writing is extremely powerful. On a daily basis, you can watch your mental judgments of situations or people you look at or talk to. You can observe your mental talk about what someone says to you or how someone looks at you. All of this information is very valuable to collect. When you see how you routinely use previously acquired and now outdated responses

ॐ

or habits, you will more likely be motivated to steer them in a new, more productive direction.

Each time you observe yourself behaving in a way that was taught to you as a child, know that it was perfect for you back then. Know that you can choose to change anything about yourself that you feel the need to change.

Each situation as it occurs is an opportunity to celebrate the observer in you doing a wonderful job. The observer becomes more and more objective and non-judgmental as the practice continues. That is what you are striving for. You will want to develop an observer who is non-judgmental and kind and allows all moments to be as they are. As time passes, the observer will become stronger, more adept at influencing your thought patterns and, thus, your actions in a fun and joyful manner. Your growth can be a joyful and glorious celebration of your Self.

Remember, it was all perfect. It is just that now you have decided to change the path. It may be time to modify something to keep the positive high Light flowing inside of you!

ॐ

65

The Root Source of Emotion

Passion has such an intense feeling. It projects outward in space and inward toward your center at the same time, thus giving it specialized power. Because it is so powerful you can learn to see the location of the emotional source of actions in others as well as in yourself.

It is important to learn to watch for this location because it will teach you that the root of all re-actions by other people, and even in yourself, really has nothing to do with you at all.

When you use your true eyes, you can see that the root of re-action is always in a state of fear. Fear cannot harm you when you send it total Love and acceptance. Even passion about a topic can be based in fear. The root wants nothing more than to be loved.

Practice finding the source of any negative action of other people as often as possible. Look for their fear and send it widening waves of Love Light. Watch what occurs when you do this. Focus on that moment and do not allow your mind to wander anywhere else.

Each moment is a perfect opportunity to find the beauty in anything you observe, touch, smell or even taste. If what you observe feels negative, send Love Life. By engaging in this type of focus you create more beauty in the world around you.

Practice this now!

🕉

66

See the Blessing in Chaos

There are many ways to determine what direction you want to follow during your stay in the Earth-level plane. Many of you feel that in some situations the choices are too many to select from and you become overwhelmed. You may feel that you do not have a choice, that you are stuck. Both perceptions can produce a tremendous amount of confusion, stress and in-action.

When you find yourself at a crossroad similar to this, first and foremost see yourself in a great and wonderful place! See the potential that is sitting at your fingertips, a potential to cause change in your

ॐ

life, an opportunity for growth into more joy! When you have been presented with a choice or even the awareness that you desire change, it means your Higher Self is nudging you. Respect the nudge and realize what is happening. Opportunity is being given by your Source!

After you center your focus on the beautiful state that change and stress can produce, then you are ready to sit, be still and observe what is truly going on. Ask for guidance and wait for your energy to perceive the proper action. You can put a thought out there and see how it makes your energy feel. Do you feel flow or stagnation? Do you feel an upward momentum or a downward flow of energy? Can you focus on the very beginning of the energy and find its total direction?

Where do you want to be in the very big picture? Ideally, how do you want to get there? Does the current decision interfere with the end goal or compliment it? Do not overlook the fact that you can find flow in most directions. The Source knows that you can grow from any experience. You need to see

ॐ

what type of flow is produced and see if it is joyful or not.

Remember, sometimes a small step in a loving supportive direction can open up a large number of positive experiences. Each moment is really a decision. Each action of thought or physical movement can cause a shift in the flow.

Start with the small thoughts, habits and actions. Focus on keeping joyful flow through these and you will see that larger opportunities will present themselves in such a way that you will know which direction to go almost automatically.

If you do not like a situation you are in, look to see if you can find the small decisions, mind patterns and actions that got you there. As you observe these in hindsight, you become more skilled in preventing the development of an uncomfortable situation.

The life path can be difficult if you rarely look at the energy of your daily decisions. That type of life will be more conducive to fluctuations of joy and peace, sadness and chaos. Practice every day keeping thoughts, actions and intentions positive, and you will

ॐ

find that the big decisions in your life will already have momentum toward joy built up behind them!

ॐ

67

View Life from the Soul Level

Why is there suffering on the Earth-level plane? Another question might be, is there really suffering or is it just part of a massive training ground for human kind? What suffers? Does the body, the spirit or the emotions of a human suffer? How is the reality of that individual actually changed?

The fact is that people choose to see life on the Earth-level plane a particular way, which leads them to have either positive enjoyable experiences or negative and fearful experiences. You can grow from both! Why choose the negative? Many people choose to learn in this way so they can't miss the punch line,

ॐ

so to speak. Perhaps in previous experiences choices were made but the effect was not perceived. In a situation such as war or mass starvation, a global consciousness sets in and takes over to set the stage for experiencing.

To enjoy a life filled with inner peace your goal becomes one of observation. You must observe all experiences from a perspective of the Soul. The Soul operates with detached observation, without judgment or malice. The Soul does this without building patterns of re-action.

So then you may ask, "What can I learn from this situation?" Be careful not to ask that question in an attempt to control future situations or outcomes. That question is valid only if it is asked so this situation is not tainted with desire or control. Just observe. Cultivating this habit can be one of the most valuable experiences you will ever need to develop. Learning will come naturally.

Don't get wrapped up in the minute or petty details of a conversation or physical action. Watch the play unfold around you. You can enjoy life much more thoroughly if you can do this consistently.

ॐ

Situations occur without your input anyway, right? So sit back, conserve your energy and watch what is going on. If you have something to share (an idea, etc.), who really wants it? Step back a moment and see the play. Then ask, "Is anyone in this room (or on this particular stage of life) really interested in what is about to come out of my mouth?"

When you think about how the Ego sees the play of life, the entire process can be quite humorous! The Ego wants to be center stage and the Soul Self wants to simply observe, to experience, and learn. You can't learn and observe from center stage; you must be off to the side to soak it all in!

ॐ

68

Reduce the Tentacles

Today you have the opportunity to find deep inside yourself the path to keep your focus either on the higher energies or the lower energies around you.

You will find that if you "check in" once in a while, you will be able to determine where your own energy is going. Where are you at this moment? Are you connected to your oneness, or do you have tentacles that are outstretched in various directions tapping into the energy of others?

If you find that you are scattered, go to the source of the reason you are in this state. The only reason you send out tentacles is that your Ego wants to be

ॐ

stimulated and made to feel energy intensely. It does not differentiate between low or high energy. It just wants intensity!

Reel the tentacles in one by one. Do this with love and respect for the topic or situation you were attracted to. Yes, deep down something was attracted to it. See the energy around each situation. Take the energy and fill it with beautiful color or patterns and see it return to the oneness. Find the next tentacle and do the same until all you have left around you is clear, balanced energy.

As you "check in" more often, you will find that you have less strayed energy strands or tentacles. Eventually, you may find that you rarely have to find a source of lower energy, because you realize what you are doing as you begin to send out a tentacle to experience lower energy.

You may meet people who keep numerous tentacles outstretched. They appear frazzled or scattered. They find it difficult to focus because they are being pulled in many directions at the same time. If you were to see them as pure energy, you would see a core area of light with little tails of light shooting away from the core in various directions. An individual in this state feels drained and frustrated. They might be able to tell you specifically what is going on, or they may say they are tired and drained all the time. The individual may be sickly or have chronic low energy.

Joy in Being comes directly from the connection with Source. An individual who is caught up in large amounts of lower energy, situations or thought patterns, will describe this Earth-level experience in more negative words than one who strives to purify the connection with the higher energy source.

Thought patterns can, by themselves, create the state of living with chronic lower energy. If one focuses on low energy thoughts over and over, they send out a vibration that looks for like energy. That is why it is important to identify any low frequency repetitive thought patterns you may have and work with them until they are resonating with a higher light and color. Find the energy as it begins, while it is still a juvenile. Do not allow it to grow and become more sophisticated.

ॐ

Checking in and acknowledging your connection repeatedly during the day is a major component to working with your Higher Self or your guides. Through this one activity, you can produce enormous change in your everyday situations.

69

Setting the Frequency in Advance

The frequency of your core energy is very important. As you become aware of your core frequency or connection, it will be easier for you to actively engage in modifying the frequency and its overtones to suit your current needs. If you choose, you can shift the direction you are headed or the situations you are attracted to and, in that manner, choose a more fulfilling, joyful and rewarding experience.

As you begin to gain continued awareness of how the situations around you influence your feelings, you will notice how situations influence what your

ॐ

frequency overtones are. This awareness will assist you to set the stage for the desired frequency of your core energy.

Do you like how you feel when you go to a particular place or see a particular person? If not, get still and send out a frequency that you do like and the similar frequencies in that person or place will resonate with yours. You can send out the frequencies with a thought of something that makes you feel good, or actually open your heart center and send out a vibration. Play with this and see what you can manifest in a room full of grumpy or stressed people! You will be pleasantly surprised how the "tone" of the room changes and how it will resonate with the part of you that is joyful.

You can set the energy prior to entering a situation you feel will be a negative experience. Set your intention to have a joyful experience and send out energy (or thoughts) to that place in advance of your arrival. As you enter the room, you will be able to feel your resonant vibration that will then be magnified as you focus on it during your visit.

ॐ

If a situation has a significant amount of non-resonant frequencies for you, it may be better to excuse yourself and ask to continue the interaction at a later time. Later, as you focus, send out the frequencies of love, patience and acceptance to the future that you will be able to "grab onto" when you enter that situation again. This will empower you to attend to the task at hand rather than focusing on your emotional survival.

The more you spread your resonant frequencies of Love and Light, the more common they will be in your environment and, over time, the less you will need to send out these frequencies in advance. You will simply walk into a comfortable set-up because you had either already been there or already thought about that area.

As you learn to take advantage of setting the tone of situations before you arrive, you will begin to attract the situations and outcomes you want rather than waiting to stumble into them. With this abundance of like, joyful, uplifting and motivating frequencies, you will find more flow and less friction

ॐ

in your everyday life. **Take charge of this one area of your life and it will influence all aspects of it.**

ॐ

70

Seeing the Oneness in All

Each of your differences reveals a unique means of connecting to Source. It gives you the opportunity to work on accomplishing your personal connections without judgment of those around you. When a difference in another is brought to your attention, you are able to see how each connection with Source is unique. This difference will aid you to see the strength of variety in the individuals on the Earth-level plane.

Call in the Light so you may see through the eyes of your Soul and no longer see yourself apart from your Brother. The concepts of differences - better,

worse, lack or abundance - are all concepts of the
Egoistic mind. In Source we are all truly one. You are
all manifesting on this plane from the same Source,
from the same Power. There are no differences, just
projections.

As you learn to see all as similar or all as one, you
know you are connected to Source. Feel the vibration
with yourself first and find it in others. Work with the
entire Earth-level plane not just humans. The plants,
animals and even the minerals have a vibration that
you should be able to identify. Practice this and learn
to carry it with you.

ॐ

71

The "Isness" of the Energy

As you grow with your new skills, you will be much more aware of the actual beauty that exists around you. You have always been able to see it, but now your sight and your focus are much more tuned into the beauty. You can see how life supports all Beings and how you are able to watch, without judgment, the manner in which life around you progresses. It makes a statement at every turn. The statement is one of "isness." How things just are and how they work and flow with perfection.

You would still contribute to "isness" even if you changed form. This is why when an animal, person or

ॐ

even a large plant changes form (or as you say, dies), the world keeps flow. Can you feel the "isness" in that statement? The world does not stop even with a huge flood or drought, earthquake or if thousands of people die all at once. The world is part of the "isness" and continues with the All-That-Is, knowing full well that energy is energy. It can never be stopped. It just changes form and continues in perfection. There is no loss or reduction when this change occurs. It is part of the whole as it always was. It is comfortable, beautiful and completely filled with Love.

When a Being changes form, the energy forms remaining are usually unable to appreciate or connect with this difference. Most people are unable to perceive the continuation of energy because the "package" has changed so drastically. They were so completely focused on the outer package that, when it no longer meets the remembered expression, loss is felt. You can grieve for another's loss of form but usually the grief is felt for yourself or the projection of loss of experience for the individual and your fear of the change of your own form.

ॐ

The Ego demands sameness. It is fighting a battle it knows it is unable to win. It enjoys the process of struggle. To know you will change form one day is something your Ego will not focus on in an effort to intensify the inevitable. This thought process keeps it a taboo subject. If one were to sit down with that fear, get comfortable, and then observe as the watcher - even view the fear from the mass consciousness - this change in form would be revealed to you from an entirely different viewpoint.

You might begin to see how there is peace, joy and fullness of action in the change of form. You can feel the "rightness" in the action when a body is no longer able to house the Source. The body is a blessing of service and education, but there are many other avenues to explore and learn. The fear of this change can mask this truth even in the individual who is embracing death.

Those aware of the energy of the individual will be able to touch this energy shift and in a moment, understand this phenomenon. The change of form is beautiful as are all stages of the flow of life force. To be able to be in a state of complete trust when this occurs to you or someone you are close to is a major accomplishment. There is joy in all situations, even as a person changes its form.

ॐ

72

Using Multiple View Points

The situations you find yourself in are brought about by your own personality, desires, beliefs and finally, your attitude at that moment. These personality influences will determine the significance and value you place on an event. You have the flexibility to expand your point of observation, which can help the situation become clearer. This clarity is achieved by using multiple viewpoints or expansion of your thoughts about a topic and may offer an alternative interpretation to work with.

The habit of seeing life situations from multiple viewpoints is what one should strive for. Allow it to

ॐ

become your norm. You see a situation occurring and, rather than having a re-action, you simply observe and consciously choose to use multiple viewpoints to help to determine your thoughts and feelings about the situation. With conscious effort and practice, one is able to do this very quickly. The more stressful the situation, the more important it is to use this technique.

Play with any situation to see if you can find a variety of responses for it. As you practice with this, you will learn that there is not a "right" way to see or understand every situation but instead they are interpreted based on your state of mind at that moment in time. The next moment may offer a uniquely different understanding of the same situation.

Persons who are able to practice this habit are able to experience life as a series of joyous experiences because they choose to find that energy in each situation.

ॐ

73

Offering Advice to Others

The Source energy is designed in such a way that one of the processes that may be used for growth is complacency. Many people are actively engaged in doing as little as possible. This in-action may draw the attention of someone who feels that it is necessary to work hard at life.

How can you know what state they exist in? How can you compare an internal state of another with yourself? You can't. It is impossible and yet many people attempt this comparison every day. There are such large variances in growth, that, as in geologic time, changes may be occurring, but the scale of time

ॐ

is enormous. This is why you as a personality are incapable of viewing a situation, be it of yourself or another, and determine its "value." The Personality Self uses the experience of one lifetime in comparisons, while the Source energy operates on a completely different scale.

Please do not become engaged in a debate over the perceived value of another's actions. There is never going to be enough information at the disposal of the Personality Self to weigh it. If you find yourself suddenly caught up in this assessment, stop and observe. Change your "view" to that of the Soul Self and your perception will change.

Remember, *it really doesn't matter.* We recommend you ask, "Does _____ really matter in the big picture?" Will you remember the situation in an hour, day, a year or ten years? Most of the time, the answer is no. All you need to do as a Personality Self is to take care of you, to become more "in the moment." This will show you how trivial even a significantly emotionally charged situation really is, to Source. How are the actions I am observing going to affect the future of humanity as a whole? Obviously this will not apply if

ॐ

someone is in danger and that person needs assistance to prevent an accident.

Remain focused in this moment and allow others to produce the best they can for the moment they are experiencing. Do this without judgment or desire to sway the outcome of the continued behavior. You have an enormous responsibility to take care of self. By detaching from the outcome of what other people do, you most optimally use your own energy. You may choose to offer love in the form of verbal advice or by example of action, but ultimately the other person will choose what he or she wants to do.

Your Personality Self becomes engaged in the desire to change others because of an Egoic interpretation of power. People manipulate others by negative means such as pouting, anger, guilt and pure force. If you manipulate someone into doing what you wanted, the real outcome of what that person did is in response to you and not because of personal growth on the part of the individual. He or she is just attempting to appease you, not develop a way of thinking.

ॐ

When you want to help someone, understand that:

- The individual may not need your input.
- You should not attach yourself to the change in behavior.

Once your comment is completed, you need to let go of the result. Move on with love, whatever the result of your effort is. If you do not, you will create chaos for your Personality Self as well as theirs.

ॐ

74

What Is Love?

Let's talk about the reality of love for a moment. If you ask 10 people what love is, you get 10 different answers. Everyone knows the word. Unlike any other word used, in any language, all ages of people will offer a definition. It is a powerful word and we all know what it is. But to capture its meaning is like holding onto a slippery fish. You think you have a solid understanding and suddenly it slips from your mind.

The reason it is difficult to define or hold onto is because of the power it represents. It can make a grown man cry tears of sadness or joy. The source of

ॐ

its power is in the Spirit. It is one of the few experiences at everyone's core. It is the very center of everyone's Being. It can consume us because it is who we really are.

Many individuals feel displaced from their Love source, forcing them to define love with words of pain, deception and defeat. Others glimpse love and define it with words of comfort, compassion and growth. Still others connect with love in such a way that they see love as a constant state of being. They feel that true love never shifts, leaves or ever wavers. People who define love in this way are able to grasp love at the Soul level or in the Soul plane. This difference in the perception of love is why people experience each situation from a different point of view.

The type of experience an individual has of Love depends on how the person connects with the Soul. It's a result of how the lens on the camera of life is focused and what is powering the camera!

True freedom comes from observing all of life through the lens of the Soul!

ॐ

75

Be Your Own Master

Oh, to dream of the times ahead of you! You may find yourself desiring the future, the change and excitement of the future. It seems so perfect, so full of possibilities and opportunities for change. Do you ever dream of a future that is exactly the same as what you have at this moment?

Why would that be a fulfilling activity? The desires deep inside you are generated as part of your core, as part of your existence in the Earth plane. You have free will, of course, but you were given this desire to move, grow and experience so that you would be less inclined to become stagnant. When you

ॐ

are sitting in one place, content and full, you don't desire change. You sit there absorbing the experience, feeling the satisfaction and basking in what you have obtained. But what does the Soul do? It, too, experiences. It was there for the struggle, for the decision to go in that particular direction, even when you were leaning in all the various directions at once. But now it, too, is looking, noticing the change and experiencing the new mental, physical and emotional shift that came with a flowing life. Soon, very soon, the Personality Self will become bored with this and begin to search for a new desire - a new path - and then it will begin making plans to initiate a new struggle or to design new goals. The new goals are necessary to fill the personality with the knowledge that all things are part of the choice and that this plane only offers the shell of experience without the meat of permanent satisfaction.

The only fulfillment is in the realization that you can continue to do Soul growth while engaged in the activities of an Earth-level life.

When you are a master of balancing your life, you are able to put appropriate importance on all of your

ॐ

activities. Put more energy into the ones that bring you joy and less energy into the difficult, painful activities. If you keep your heart open to your Soul's guidance, balance will be at your center.

Balance is one of the most powerful states to create.

ॐ

Glossary

All-That-Is

> This refers to the highest form of energy; Consciousness of the Universe.

Being

> A term used to describe the current state of an entity.

Centered

> A state of being when the Personality Self is connected to the energy flow of the Universe.

Consciousness

> A term used to describe the human connection to the all-knowing source of energy. The Soul Self is also used to describe this relationship in a more personal manner.

ॐ

Downward Flow

A state of energy flow that increases the gap of the connection with the Universal flow.

Egoic Self

The part of you that is connected to the energy of mankind. This part of you focuses on survival and obtaining a constant flow of intense energy.

Energy Body

The entire history of an individual's energy patterns housed inside and outside the physical form.

Fluid

A state of being when an individual is able to maintain the connection with the Universe while actively engaged in daily Earth-level plane activities.

Fog

A thought pattern that decreases the ability of an individual to see a situation clearly.

ॐ

Higher Self

The part of the Personality Self that is able to connect with the Soul Self.

Isness

The pure energy behind all thought, action and creation. The energy behind the outcome of any situation.

Maintaining the Connection

A state of being in which one is fluid with the intent to combine the world of spirit with the world of physical.

Mantra

A series of words, thoughts, even music, used to calm the Personality Self and connect with upward flow energy.

ॐ

Personality Self

> The part of you that you develop since the day you are born. The Personality Self is the habits, traits and behaviors that you use to survive the day-to-day activities in the Earth plane.

Re-active Behavior

> A learned (self-taught) action in response to a situation or action of another. It can be a present situation or re-lived (memory) situation.

Soul Self

> The individual's energy body that is part of Consciousness.

Source

> A name of the highest frequency of Being; Consciousness.

Spirit

> A term used to describe Consciousness.

ॐ

Universe

A term used to describe the Consciousness of All-That-Is.

Upward Flow

A state of energy flow that decreases the gap of the connection with the Universal flow.

Watchtower

A carefully created mental awareness designed to alert the user when the current thoughts or actions are in the direction of downward flow energy. This state then offers a place to regroup the energy.

Your path

The direction your Earth-level life has taken as the result of the daily choices you have made.

ॐ

www.ingramcontent.com/pod-product-compliance
Lightning Source LLC
LaVergne TN
LVHW051503080426
835509LV00017B/1890